THE CONDEMNED OF ALTONA

A Play in Five Acts

THE
CONDEMNED
OF ALTONA

A Play in Five Acts

by

JEAN-PAUL SARTRE

TRANSLATED FROM THE FRENCH BY
Sylvia and George Leeson

The Norton Library
W·W·NORTON & COMPANY·INC·
NEW YORK

Originally published in French as *Les Séquestrés D'Altona,* © 1960 Librairie Gallimard.
Published in Great Britain as LOSER WINS by Hamish Hamilton, Ltd.

W. W. Norton & Company, Inc. also publishes *The Norton Anthology of English Literature,*
edited by M. H. Abrams et al; *The Norton Anthology of Poetry,* edited by Arthur M.
Eastman et al; *World Masterpieces,* edited by Maynard Mack et al; *The Norton Reader,*
edited by Arthur M. Eastman et al, *The Norton Facsimile of the First Folio of Shakespeare,*
prepared by Charlton Hinman; *The Norton Anthology of Modern Poetry,* edited by Richard
Ellmann and Robert O'Clair; and the *Norton Critical Editions.*

Library of Congress Cataloging in Publication Data

Sartre, Jean Paul, 1905–
The Condemned of Altona.

(The Norton Library)
Translation of Les Séquestrés d'Altona.
I. Title.
PQ2637.A82S43   1978   842'.9'14   78-1059

ISBN 13: 978-0-393-00889-0

1 2 3 4 5 6 7 8 9 0

I thought that I had invented the name Gerlach. I was mistaken. It was hidden in my memory. I regret my mistake even more because the name is that of one of the bravest and best-known opponents of National Socialism.

Hellmuth von Gerlach devoted his life to the struggle for *rapprochement* between France and Germany, and for peace. In 1933 his name was high up in the list of those proscribed by the Nazis. His property was seized, together with that of his family. He died in exile two years later, having devoted his last efforts to providing help for his refugee compatriots.

It is too late to change the names of my characters, but I beg his friends and relatives to accept this as an earnest of my apology and my regret.

ACT I

A large room crowded with pretentious ugly furniture,
most of which is in the German style of the end of
the nineteenth century. An inside staircase leads to a
small landing. On the landing, a closed door. Two
French windows, right, lead to a thickly wooded
park; the light filtering in through the trees has a
greenish hue. Upstage, right and left, two doors. On
the wall upstage, three enormous photographs of
Franz, mourning crape draped on the frames at the
bottom and on the right.

LENI is standing, WERNER is seated in an armchair, while
JOHANNA is seated on a settee. They are silent. Then,
after a moment, the large German clock strikes three.
WERNER jumps up. LENI bursts into laughter.

LENI: Attention! (Pause.) At thirty-three! (Annoyed)
Oh, sit down!

JOHANNA: Why? Isn't it time?

LENI: Time? Now we start waiting, that's all. (WERNER
shrugs his shoulders. To WERNER) You know very
well we shall have to wait.

JOHANNA: How should he know?

LENI: Because it's the rule. At all family confer-
ences . . .

JOHANNA: Have there been many?

LENI: They were our big occasions.

JOHANNA: I hope you enjoyed them.

LENI (*continuing*): Werner was always early, and old Hindenburg always late.

WERNER (*to* JOHANNA): Don't believe a word of it. Father has always done things with military precision.

LENI: Absolutely! We used to wait here while he smoked a cigar in his office and looked at his watch. At three ten he would make his entry, military fashion. Ten minutes; not a minute more, not a minute less. Twelve at staff meetings, eight when he presided at meetings of the directors.

JOHANNA: Why go to all that trouble?

LENI: To give us time to be afraid.

JOHANNA: And down at the shipyard?

LENI: The boss arrives last.

JOHANNA (*amazed*): What? Who says that? (*She laughs.*) No one believes that any more.

LENI: Old Hindenburg believed it for fifty years of his life.

JOHANNA: Perhaps so, but now . . .

LENI: Now, he no longer believes in anything. (*Pause.*) Nevertheless, he'll be ten minutes late. Principles may go, habits remain. Bismarck was still alive when our poor father acquired his habits. (*To* WERNER) Don't you remember how we waited? (*To* JOHANNA) He used to tremble and wonder who was going to be punished.

WERNER: Didn't you tremble, Leni?

LENI (*laughing dryly*): Me? I used to die of fright, but I used to say to myself: he'll pay for it.

JOHANNA (*ironically*): Has he paid?

LENI (*smiling, but very harsh*): He is paying. (*She turns to* WERNER.) Who's going to be punished,

Werner? Which of us two? How it makes us young again! (*Suddenly fierce*) I hate victims who respect their executioners.

JOHANNA: Werner is not a victim.

LENI: Look at him!

JOHANNA (*pointing to the mirror*): Look at yourself!

LENI (*surprised*): Me?

JOHANNA: You don't look so good. And you're talking a lot.

LENI: That's just to distract you. It's a long time since I've been afraid of father. Anyway, this time we know what he's going to say.

WERNER: I haven't the slightest idea.

LENI: Not the slightest? Hypocrite! Pharisee! You close your eyes to everything unpleasant! (*To* JOHANNA) Old Hindenburg is going to die, Johanna. Didn't you know?

JOHANNA: Yes, I did.

WERNER: It's not true. (*He starts to tremble.*) I tell you it's not true.

LENI: Stop trembling! (*Suddenly violent*) Die, yes, die! Like a dog! And you were told. The proof of that is that you told everything to Johanna.

JOHANNA: You're wrong, Leni.

LENI: Go on! He has no secrets from you.

JOHANNA: Oh, yes, he has some.

LENI: Then who told you?

JOHANNA: You.

LENI (*stunned*): Me?

JOHANNA: Three weeks ago one of the doctors came to see you in the Blue Room after the consultation.

LENI: Hilbert, yes. What of it?

JOHANNA: I met you in the corridor. He had just gone.

LENI: Well?

JOHANNA: Nothing. (*Pause.*) Your face gives you away, Leni.

LENI: I didn't know that. Thank you. Did I look elated?

JOHANNA: You looked terrified.

LENI (*shouts*): That's not true! (*She regains control of herself.*)

JOHANNA (*gently*): Go and look at your face in the mirror. The terror is still there.

LENI (*curtly*): I'll leave the looking glasses to you.

WERNER (*striking the arm of his chair*): That's enough! (*He looks at them angrily.*) If it's true that father is going to die, have the decency to keep quiet. (*To* LENI) What's the matter with him? (*She does not reply.*) I'm asking you what's the matter with him.

LENI: You know.

WERNER: That's not true.

LENI: You knew twenty minutes before I did.

JOHANNA: Leni, what are you trying to . . . ?

LENI: Before going to the Blue Room, Hilbert went through the Rose Room. He met my brother and told him everything.

JOHANNA (*amazed*): Werner! (*He slumps down into the armchair without replying.*) I—I don't understand.

LENI: You still don't know the Gerlachs, Johanna.

JOHANNA (*pointing to* WERNER): I knew one in Hamburg three years ago, and I fell in love with him right away. He was free, he was open, and he was gay. How you have changed him!

LENI: Was he afraid of words in Hamburg, your Gerlach?

JOHANNA: No, he wasn't.

LENI: It's here that he's really himself.

JOHANNA (*turning to* WERNER *sadly*): You lied to me!

WERNER (*sharply*): Not another word. (*Pointing to*
LENI) Look at her smile. She's preparing the ground.

JOHANNA: For whom?

WERNER: For father. We are the chosen victims, and
their first aim is to separate us. Whatever you may
think, don't reproach me. You would be playing their
game.

JOHANNA (*tender, but serious*): I have nothing to reproach you with.

WERNER (*wildly*): That's all right, then! That's all
right, then!

JOHANNA: What do they want of us?

WERNER: Don't worry, they'll tell us. (*Pause.*)

JOHANNA: What's wrong with him?

LENI: Who?

JOHANNA: Father.

LENI: Cancer of the throat.

JOHANNA: Does one die of it?

LENI: Usually. (*Pause.*) He may drag on. (*Quietly*)
You used to like him, didn't you?

JOHANNA: I still do.

LENI: He was always attractive to women. (*Pause.*)
What a retribution! That mouth which was so loved
. . . (*She sees that* JOHANNA *does not understand.*)
Perhaps you don't know, but cancer of the throat
has this great disadvantage—

JOHANNA (*She understands.*): Be quiet!

LENI: You are becoming a Gerlach. Bravo!
(*She goes to get the Bible, a thick, heavy sixteenth-
century volume, and carries it with difficulty to the
pedestal table.*)

JOHANNA: What's that?

LENI: The Bible. We put it on the table when we hold
a family conference. (JOHANNA *looks at it, aston-*

ished. LENI *adds, a trifle impatiently*) Yes, in case we
have to take an oath.

JOHANNA: There's no oath to take.

LENI: You never know.

JOHANNA (*laughing to reassure herself*): You believe
neither in God nor the Devil.

LENI: That's true. But we go to church, and we swear
on the Bible. I've already told you—this family has
no longer any justification for living, but it has kept
its good habits. (*She looks at the clock.*) Ten past
three, Werner. You can stand up.

(*At that moment the* FATHER *enters by the French
window.* WERNER *hears the door open and turns
around.* JOHANNA *hesitates before standing, but at
last does so with bad grace. The* FATHER, *however,
walks quickly across the room and places his hands on
her shoulders to make her sit down again.*)

FATHER: Please, my child. (*She sits down again; he
bows, kisses her hand, straightens up rather quickly,
and looks at* WERNER *and* LENI.) Well, I don't need
to tell you, do I? Very good! Let's get to the point,
and without ceremony, eh? (*Brief silence.*) So, I am
condemned. (WERNER *takes his arm, but he pulls
away almost brutally.*) I said—without ceremony.
(WERNER, *hurt, turns away and sits down again. Pause.
The* FATHER *looks at all three and speaks in a slightly
harsh voice.*) How unconcernedly you all take my
death! (*Keeping his eyes on them, as though to convince them*) I am going to die. I am going to die.
There's no doubt about it. (*He recovers himself. Almost playful*) My children, Nature is playing me a
shabby trick. Whatever my worth, this body of mine
never harmed anyone. In six months I shall have all
the disadvantages of a corpse without any of its

advantages. (*At a gesutre from* WERNER, *he laughs.*)
Sit down! I shall go decently.

LENI (*politely interested*): You are going . . .

FATHER: Do you think I shall submit to the extrav-
agance of a few cells, I who set steel afloat on the
seas? (*Short pause.*) Six months is more than I need
to put my affairs in order.

WERNER: And after the six months?

FATHER: After? What do you think? Nothing.

LENI: Nothing at all?

FATHER: An industrial casualty. Things restored to their
natural order.

WERNER (*in a choked voice*): By whom?

FATHER: By you, if you are capable of it. (WERNER
starts. The FATHER *laughs.*) Don't worry, I'll take
care of everything. You will only have to worry about
the funeral arrangements. (*Pause.*) Enough of that.
(*Long pause. To* JOHANNA, *pleasantly*) My child, I
ask you to be patient just a little longer. (*To* LENI
and WERNER, *changing his tone*) You will have to
swear an oath, one after the other.

JOHANNA (*anxious*): What ceremony! And you said
you didn't want any. What is there to swear?

FATHER (*good-humoredly*): Nothing much, daughter-
in-law. In any case, in-laws are exempt from the
oath. (*He turns toward his son with a solemnity that
could be taken as ironic or sincere.*) Werner, stand
up! You were a lawyer, my son. When Franz died, I
called on you for help, and you left the Bar without
hesitation. That deserves a reward. You will be
master of this house and head of the firm. (*To*
JOHANNA) You see, nothing to worry about. I am
making him one of the kings of this world. (JOHANNA
remains silent.) Don't you agree?

JOHANNA: It's not for me to answer you.

FATHER: Werner! (*Impatiently*) You refuse?

WERNER (*gloomy and troubled*): I shall do what you wish.

FATHER: Of course you will. (*He looks at him.*) But you are reluctant to do it?

WERNER: Yes.

FATHER: The largest shipbuilding firm is handed to you and that breaks your heart. Why?

WERNER: I— Let's say I'm not worthy of it.

FATHER: That's quite probable. But I can't help it. You are my sole male heir.

WERNER: Franz had all the necessary qualities.

FATHER: Except one, since he is dead.

WERNER: You see, I was a good lawyer. I shall find it hard to resign myself to being a bad employer.

FATHER: Perhaps you won't be such a bad one.

WERNER: When I look a man in the eyes I become incapable of giving him orders.

FATHER: Why?

WERNER: I feel that he is my equal.

FATHER. Look at him above the eyes. (*He touches his forehead.*) There, for example. That's only bone.

WERNER: I should need your pride.

FATHER: Haven't you got it?

WERNER: Where could I have got it from? You spared nothing to mold Franz in your own image. Is it my fault that you taught me nothing but passive obedience?

FATHER: It's the same thing.

WERNER: What? What's the same thing?

FATHER: To obey and to command. In both cases you transmit orders you have received.

WERNER: You receive orders?

FATHER: Up to quite recently, I did.

WERNER: From whom?

FATHER: I don't know. Myself, perhaps. (*Smiling*) I'll give you the formula. If you want to command, think of yourself as someone else.

WERNER: I can't think of myself as anyone else.

FATHER: Wait till I die. At the end of a week you will think you are me.

WERNER: To decide! To decide! To be responsible for everything. Alone. On behalf of a hundred thousand men. And you have managed to live!

FATHER: It's a long time since I have decided anything. I sign the correspondence. Next year you will sign it.

WERNER: Don't you do anything else?

FATHER: Nothing for nearly ten years.

WERNER: Why are you needed? Wouldn't anyone do?

FATHER: Yes, anyone.

WERNER: Me, for example.

FATHER: You, for example.

WERNER: Nothing is perfect. There are so many cogs in the machine. Suppose one of them were to jam. . . .

FATHER: For repairs, Gelber will be there. A remarkable man, you know, who has been with us for twenty-five years.

WERNER: I'm lucky, in fact. He will give the orders.

FATHER: Gelber? You're mad! He is your employee. You pay him to let you know what orders to give.

WERNER (*after a pause*): Oh, father, not once in your life have you trusted me. You thrust me at the head of the firm because I am your sole male heir, but you first made sure of turning me into an ornament.

FATHER (*laughing sadly*): An ornament! And I? What am I? A hat on a flagpole. (*With a sad and gentle air, almost senile*) The greatest enterprise in Europe

. . . It's quite an organization, isn't it? Quite an organization.

WERNER: Perfect. If I find time hangs heavily, I'll go back to law. And we shall travel too.

FATHER: No.

WERNER (*astonished*): It's the best thing I could do.

FATHER (*imperious and crushing*): Out of the question. (*He looks at* WERNER *and* LENI.) Now listen to me. The estate is to remain intact. You are strictly forbidden to sell or hand over your share to anyone whatsoever. You are forbidden to sell this house. You are forbidden to leave it. You will live in it until you die. Swear! (*To* LENI) You first.

LENI (*smiling*): To be honest, I must remind you that I am not bound by oaths.

FATHER (*also smiling*): Go on, Leni, I rely on you. Be an example to your brother.

(LENI *approaches the Bible and raises her hand. She fights against an overwhelming desire to laugh.*)

LENI: I . . . Oh, what does it matter! Excuse me, father, but I can't help laughing. (*Aside to* JOHANNA) It happens every time.

FATHER (*good-humored*): Laugh, my child. I only ask you to swear.

LENI (*smiling*): I swear on the Holy Bible to obey your last wishes. (*The* FATHER *looks at her, laughing, then turns to* WERNER.) Your turn, head of the family.

(WERNER *appears lost in thought.*)

FATHER: Well, Werner?

(WERNER *raises his head sharply and looks at his father with a haunted look.*)

LENI (*serious*): Deliver us, brother. Swear, and all will be over.

(WERNER *turns toward the Bible.*)

JOHANNA (*courteously and quietly*): One moment, please. (*The* FATHER *looks at her, feigning amazement in order to intimidate her. She returns his gaze without emotion.*) Leni's oath was a farce. Everyone laughed. When Werner's turn comes, no one laughs any more. Why?

LENI: Because your husband takes everything seriously.

JOHANNA: One more reason to laugh. (*Pause.*) You were watching him, Leni.

FATHER (*with authority*): Johanna . . .

JOHANNA: You too, father, you were watching him.

LENI: Well, you were watching me also.

JOHANNA: Father, I wish we were frank with each other.

FATHER: You and I?

JOHANNA: You and I. (*The* FATHER *smiles.* JOHANNA *takes the Bible and carries it with difficulty to another table, farther away.*) First, let's talk. Then whoever wants to swear may do so.

LENI: Werner! Are you going to let your wife defend you?

WERNER: Am I being attacked, then?

JOHANNA (*to the* FATHER): I should like to know why you dispose of my life.

FATHER (*pointing to* WERNER): I dispose of his because it belongs to me, but I have no power over yours.

JOHANNA (*smiling*): Do you think we have two lives? You were married. Did you love their mother?

FATHER: I loved her as a husband should.

JOHANNA (*smiling*): I see, and she died of it. We love each other more than that, father. We always decided everything that concerned us, together. (*Pause*). If he swears under constraint, if he shuts himself up in this house in order to remain faithful to his vow, he will decide without me and against me. You will separate us forever.

FATHER (*with a smile*): Don't you like our house?

JOHANNA: Not in the least.

(*Pause.*)

FATHER: What don't you like, daughter-in-law?

JOHANNA: I married a lawyer in Hamburg who possessed only his talent. Three years later I find myself in the solitude of this fortress, married to a shipbuilder.

FATHER: Is that such a miserable fate?

JOHANNA: For me, yes. I loved Werner for his independence, and you know very well that he has lost it.

FATHER: Who has taken it from him?

JOHANNA: You.

FATHER: Eighteen months ago you decided to come and settle here.

JOHANNA: You asked us to.

FATHER: Well, if a wrong has been done, you share the blame.

JOHANNA: I didn't want him to have to choose between you and me.

FATHER: You were wrong.

LENI (*amiably*): He would have chosen you.

JOHANNA: An even chance. A hundred-per-cent chance that he would have hated his choice.

FATHER: Why?

JOHANNA: Because he loves you. (*The* FATHER *shrugs his shoulders irritably.*) Do you know what a hopeless love is like? (*The* FATHER's *expression changes.* LENI *notices it.*)

LENI (*quickly*): And you, Johanna, do you know?

JOHANNA (*coldly*): No. (*Pause.*) Werner knows.

(ᴡᴇʀɴᴇʀ *gets up and walks toward the French win-dow.*)

ꜰᴀᴛʜᴇʀ (*to* ᴡᴇʀɴᴇʀ): Where are you going?

ᴡᴇʀɴᴇʀ: I'm going out. You'll be more comfortable.

ᴊᴏʜᴀɴɴᴀ: Werner! I am fighting for *us.*

ᴡᴇʀɴᴇʀ: For us? (*Very curtly*) At the Gerlachs' the women keep quiet. (*He is about to go out.*)

ꜰᴀᴛʜᴇʀ (*softly, but imperiously*): Werner! (ᴡᴇʀɴᴇʀ *stops dead.*) Come back and sit down.
(ᴡᴇʀɴᴇʀ *slowly returns to his seat, turns his back on them, and buries his head in his hands as though to indicate that he refuses to take part in the conversation.*)

ᴡᴇʀɴᴇʀ: Talk to Johanna!

ꜰᴀᴛʜᴇʀ: Good! Well, daughter-in-law?

ᴊᴏʜᴀɴɴᴀ (*with an anxious look at* ᴡᴇʀɴᴇʀ): Let's postpone this interview. I am very tired.

ꜰᴀᴛʜᴇʀ: No, my child. You began it. We must finish it. (*Pause.* ᴊᴏʜᴀɴɴᴀ, *at a loss, looks at* ᴡᴇʀɴᴇʀ *in silence.*) Am I to understand that you refuse to live here after my death?

ᴊᴏʜᴀɴɴᴀ (*almost pleading*): Werner! (ᴡᴇʀɴᴇʀ *remains silent. She abruptly changes her attitude.*) Yes, father, that's what I mean.

ꜰᴀᴛʜᴇʀ: Where will you live?

ᴊᴏʜᴀɴɴᴀ: In our old apartment.

ꜰᴀᴛʜᴇʀ: You'll return to Hamburg?

ᴊᴏʜᴀɴɴᴀ: We shall return there.

ʟᴇɴɪ: If Werner wants to.

ᴊᴏʜᴀɴɴᴀ: He will.

ꜰᴀᴛʜᴇʀ: And the firm? Do you agree to his being head of the firm?

ᴊᴏʜᴀɴɴᴀ: Yes, if that is your wish and if Werner has a taste for playing at being a figurehead.

FATHER (*as if thinking the matter over*): Live in Hamburg . . .

JOHANNA (*hopefully*): We ask nothing else. Won't you make this single concession to us?

FATHER (*friendly but adamant*): No. (*Pause.*) My son will stay here, to live and die here as I am doing and my father and grandfather did.

JOHANNA: Why?

FATHER: Why not?

JOHANNA: Does the house have to be lived in?

FATHER: Yes.

JOHANNA (*violently*): Then let it collapse!

(LENI *bursts into laughter.*)

LENI (*politely*): Would you like me to set fire to it? It was one of my childhood dreams.

FATHER (*glancing around in amusement*): Poor house, does it deserve such hatred? Is it Werner who finds it so horrible?

JOHANNA: Werner and me. How ugly it is!

LENI: We know that.

JOHANNA: There are four of us. At the end of the year there will be three. Do we need thirty-two cluttered rooms? When Werner is at the yard I am afraid.

FATHER: And so that's why you want to leave us? They are not serious reasons.

JOHANNA: No.

FATHER: Are there others?

JOHANNA: Yes.

FATHER: Let's have them.

WERNER (*shouting*): Johanna, I forbid you. . . .

JOHANNA: Well, speak for yourself!

WERNER: What's the good? You know very well I shall obey him.

JOHANNA: Why?

WERNER: He's my father. Oh, let's have done with it.
(*He stands up.*)

JOHANNA (*placing herself in front of him*): No,
Werner, no!

FATHER: He is right, daughter-in-law. Let us have done
with it. A family is a house. I ask *you* to live in this
house because you have become part of our family.

JOHANNA (*laughing*): The family has a broad back,
and you are not sacrificing us to it.

FATHER: To whom, then?

JOHANNA: To your elder son!
(*Long pause.*)

LENI (*calmly*): Franz died in the Argentine nearly four
years ago. (JOHANNA *laughs in her face.*) We received
the death certificate in fifty-six. Go to the Altona
Town Hall. They will show it to you.

JOHANNA: Dead? I should think so. What else could
you call the life he leads? One thing is sure: dead
or alive, he is in this house.

LENI: No.

JOHANNA (*pointing to the door on the first floor*): Up
there. Behind that door.

LENI: What madness! Who told you that?
(*Pause.* WERNER *rises quietly. From the time that the
subject of his brother comes up, his eyes shine and
he recovers his confidence.*)

WERNER: Who do you think? I did.

LENI: In bed?

JOHANNA: Why not?

LENI: Phew!

WERNER: She's my wife. She has the right to know what
I know.

LENI: The right of love? How insipid you are! I would
give my body and soul to the man I loved, but I

would lie to him all my life if it were necessary.

WERNER (*violently*): Listen to this blind woman who speaks of colors. Who would you lie to? To parrots?

FATHER (*in a commanding voice*): Be quiet, all three of you. (*He strokes* LENI's *hair.*) The skull is hard, but the hair is soft. (*She pulls away brutally. He remains alert.*) Franz has lived upstairs for thirteen years. He does not leave his room, and no one sees him except Leni, who looks after him.

WERNER: And you.

FATHER: I? Who told you that? Leni? And you believed her? How close the two of you get when anything is likely to hurt you, Werner. It is thirteen years since I last saw him.

WERNER (*stunned*): But why?

FATHER (*very matter-of-fact*): Because he won't see me.

WERNER (*taken aback*): Good. (*Pause.*) Good. (*He returns to his seat.*)

FATHER (*to* JOHANNA): Thank you, my child. In the family, you see, we have no objection to the truth. But whenever possible we contrive to have it spoken by a stranger. (*Pause.*) So, Franz lives up there, alone and ill. Does that change anything?

JOHANNA: Almost everything. (*Pause.*) Don't worry, father. An in-law, a stranger, will speak the truth for you. This is what I know. A scandal broke out in forty-six. I don't know what it was, since my husband was a prisoner in France at the time. It appears there were legal proceedings. Franz disappeared—you say to the Argentine. Actually, he hid himself here. In fifty-six, Gelber made a quick trip to South America and brought back a death certificate. Some time after, you ordered Werner to give up his career, and you installed him here as your heir. Am I wrong?

FATHER: No. Continue.

JOHANNA: I have nothing more to say. Who Franz was, what he did, what has become of him, I do not know. The only thing I am certain of is that if we remain, it will be to become slaves to him.

LENI (*fiercely*): That's not true! He needs only me.

JOHANNA: I can't believe that.

LENI: He won't see anyone but me!

JOHANNA: That may be, but in the background father protects him, and later we shall have to protect him. Or guard him. Perhaps we shall be his slaves and his jailers.

LENI (*outraged*): Am I his jailer?

JOHANNA: How do I know? Supposing the two of you had locked him up?

(*Pause.* LENI *takes a key from her pocket.*)

LENI: Go upstairs and knock. If he doesn't open the door, here's the key.

JOHANNA (*taking the key*): Thank you. (*She looks at* WERNER.) What should I do, Werner?

WERNER: What you like. One way or another, you will see that it is a booby trap. . . .

(JOHANNA *hesitates, then slowly climbs the stairs and knocks at the door. Once, twice. A kind of nervous fury takes possession of her. A rain of blows against the door. She turns toward the room and is about to descend.*)

LENI (*quietly*): You have the key. (*Pause.* JOHANNA *hesitates. She is afraid.* WERNER *is anxious and agitated.* JOHANNA *masters herself, inserts the key in the lock, turns it, and tries vainly to open the door.*) Well?

JOHANNA: There is an inside bolt. It must be fastened. (*She starts to come down.*)

LENI: Who fastened it? Did I?

JOHANNA: Perhaps there is another door.

LENI: You know very well there is not. This house is isolated. If anyone has bolted it, it can only be Franz. (JOHANNA *has reached the foot of the staircase.*) Well, are we holding him prisoner?

JOHANNA: There are many ways of holding a man prisoner. The best is to get him to imprison himself.

LENI: How does one do that?

JOHANNA: By lying to him. (*She looks at* LENI, *who appears disconcerted.*)

FATHER (*to* WERNER, quickly): Have you acted as counsel in cases of this kind?

WERNER: What kind?

FATHER: Illegal restraint.

WERNER (*in a choked voice*): Once.

FATHER: Good. Suppose the premises were searched. The court would institute proceedings, would it not?

WERNER (*trapped*): Why should there be a search? There never has been one in thirteen years.

FATHER: I have been here. (*Pause.*)

LENI (*to* JOHANNA): And then you've told me I drive too fast. I could crash into a tree. What would become of Franz?

JOHANNA: If he is in his right mind, he will call the servants.

LENI: He is in his right mind, but he will not call them. (*Pause.*) They will discover my brother's death by the smell! (*Pause.*) They will break down the door and find him on the floor among the shells.

JOHANNA: What shells?

LENI: He likes oysters.

FATHER (*to* JOHANNA, *in a friendly manner*): Listen to

her. If he dies, it will be the scandal of the century, Johanna. . . .

JOHANNA (*in a hard voice*): Why should you care? You'll be under the ground.

FATHER (*smiling*): I shall, yes. But not you. Let us go back to that affair in forty-six. Would there be a statute of limitations? Answer! It's your profession.

WERNER: I don't know the offense.

FATHER: At best, assault and battery; at the worst, attempted murder.

WERNER (*in a choked voice*): There would be no statute of limitations.

FATHER: You know what we can expect—complicity in attempted murder, forgery and the use of forged documents, and illegal restraint.

WERNER: Forgery? What forgery?

FATHER (*laughs*): The death certificate, of course! It cost me plenty. (*Pause.*) What do you say, lawyer? The Criminal Court?

(WERNER *is silent.*)

JOHANNA: Werner, the game's up. It's up to us to choose. We shall either be servants of the madman whom they prefer to you, or we shall stand in the dock. What is your choice? Mine is made. The Criminal Court. I'd prefer a term in prison to penal servitude for life. (*Pause.*) Well?

(WERNER *says nothing. She makes a gesture of discouragement.*)

FATHER (*warmly*): Children, I am thunderstruck. Blackmail! Traps! It all sounds false. It is all forced. My son, I am only asking for a little pity for your brother. There are situations that Leni cannot deal with alone. For the rest, you will be as free as air. You will see. Everything will turn out all right. Franz will not live very long, I fear. One night you will bury him in the park. With him will disappear the last of the *true* Von Gerlachs. . . . (*At a gesture from* WERNER) I mean the last monster. You are both sane and normal. You will have normal children who will live where they wish. Stay, Johanna, for the sake of Werner's sons. They will inherit the firm. It is a fabulous power, and you haven't the right to deprive them of it.

WERNER (*starting, his eyes hard and glittering*): Eh? (*They all look at him.*) Did you really say: for Werner's sons? (*The* FATHER, *astonished, nods.* WERNER *continues triumphantly.*) There it is, Johanna, there's the trick. Werner and his children. Father, you don't give a damn for them. You don't give a damn! You don't give a damn! (JOHANNA *goes up to him. Pause.*) Even if you were to live long enough to see my first son, he would loathe you because he would be flesh of my flesh and because I have been filled with loathing for you from the day I was born. (*To* JOHANNA) Poor father! What a mess! He would have adored Franz's children.

JOHANNA (*urgently*): Stop! You should hear yourself. We are lost if you pity yourself.

WERNER: On the contrary. I am freeing myself. What do you want me to do? Turn them down flat?

JOHANNA: Yes.

WERNER (*laughs*): That's fine!

JOHANNA: Tell them *no*. Without shouting, without laughing. Just plain no.

(WERNER *turns toward the* FATHER *and* LENI. *They look at him in silence.*)

WERNER: They are looking at me.

JOHANNA: What of it? (WERNER *shrugs his shoulders and goes to sit down. With extreme weariness*) Werner! (*He does not look at her any more. Long silence.*)

FATHER (*discreetly triumphant*): Well, daughter-in-law?

JOHANNA: He has not sworn.

FATHER: He will. The weak serve the strong. That's the law.

JOHANNA (*hurt*): Who is strong according to you? The one upstairs, half mad and more helpless than a babe in arms, or my husband whom you abandoned and who has managed quite well on his own?

FATHER: Werner is weak, Franz is strong. That can't be helped.

JOHANNA: What do the strong do on this earth?

FATHER: In general, they do nothing.

JOHANNA: I see.

FATHER: They are people who, by nature, live in close intimacy with death. They hold the destiny of others in their hands.

JOHANNA: Is Franz like that?

FATHER: Yes.

JOHANNA: What do you know about him after thirteen years?

FATHER: He holds the destiny of all four of us here in his hands without even thinking of it.

JOHANNA: What does he think of, then?

LENI (*ironic and brutal, but frank*): Crabs.

JOHANNA (*ironic*): All day long?

LENI: It is very absorbing.

JOHANNA: What old-fashioned nonsense! As old as your furniture. Go on! You don't believe in it.

FATHER (*smiling*): I have only six months to live,

daughter-in-law. It is too short a time to believe in anything. (*Pause.*) Werner believes it, though.

WERNER: You are mistaken, father. Those were your ideas, not mine, and you instilled them into me. But since you have lost them on the way, you shouldn't take it amiss that I have rid myself of them. I am like any other man. Neither strong nor weak, and, like anyone else, I am trying to live. As for Franz, I don't know whether I'd still recognize him, but I'm sure he's like anyone else. (*He shows* FRANZ's *photographs to* JOHANNA.) What does he have that I haven't? (*He looks at them, fascinated.*) He's not even handsome.

LENI (*ironic*): No! Not even!

WERNER (*still fascinated, weakening already*): And what if I had been born to serve him? There are slaves who revolt. My brother will not be my destiny.

LENI: Do you prefer that your wife should be?

JOHANNA: Do you consider me one of the strong?

LENI: Yes.

JOHANNA: What a strange idea! Why?

LENI: You were an actress, weren't you? A star?

JOHANNA: Yes, I was. But my career was a failure. What else?

LENI: What else? Well, you married Werner; since then you have done nothing, and you think of death.

JOHANNA: If you seek to humiliate him, you are wasting your time. When he met me, I had left the stage for good. I was out of my mind. He can be proud of having saved me.

LENI: I bet he isn't.

JOHANNA (*to* WERNER): What do you say?
(*Pause.* WERNER *does not reply.*)

LENI: How you embarrass the poor man. (*Pause.*)

Johanna, would you have chosen him if you hadn't failed? Some marriages are funerals.

(JOHANNA *is about to reply, but the* FATHER *intervenes.*)

FATHER: Leni! (*He strokes her hair. She dodges away angrily.*) You surpass yourself, my girl. If I were vain, I should believe that my death upsets you.

LENI (*quickly*): You needn't doubt that, father. You can see very well that she'll throw a wrench in the works.

FATHER (*starting to laugh; to* JOHANNA): Don't be angry with Leni, my child. She means that we are of the same species: you, Franz, and I. (*Pause.*) I like you, Johanna, and at times I have felt that you would mourn my death. You will certainly be the only one. (*He smiles at her.*)

JOHANNA (*bluntly*): If you still care about life, and if it is my good fortune that you like me, how do you dare humiliate my husband in front of me? (*The* FATHER *shakes his head without replying.*) Are you on this side of death?

FATHER: This side, the other side. It makes no difference any more. Six months—I am an old man with no future. (*He looks into space and speaks to himself.*) The firm will continue to grow. Private investment won't be enough. The State will have to stick its nose in. Franz will remain upstairs for ten years, twenty years. He will suffer. . . .

LENI (*dogmatically*): He does not suffer.

FATHER (*not hearing her*): Death for me is now merely the continuation of my life without me. (*Pause. He sits down and, huddled in his chair, stares fixedly into space.*) He will have gray hair . . . the unhealthy fat of prisoners. . . .

LENI (*fiercely*): Be quiet!

FATHER (*not hearing*): It is intolerable. (*He appears to be suffering.*)

WERNER (*slowly*): Would you feel any happier if we stayed here?

JOHANNA (*quickly*): Take care!

WERNER: Of what? He's my father. I don't want him to suffer.

JOHANNA: He is suffering for the other one.

.WERNER: I don't care.

(*He goes for the Bible and brings it back to the table on which* LENI *had placed it before.*)

JOHANNA (*quickly*): He's putting it on for your benefit.

WERNER (*ill-natured, his voice full of innuendo*): And you? Aren't you doing the same thing? (*To the* FATHER) Answer. . . . Would you be any happier . . . ?

FATHER: I don't know.

WERNER (*to the* FATHER): We'll see. (*Pause. The* FATHER *and* LENI *make no sign. They wait, watching keenly.*)

JOHANNA: One question. Just one question, and then you can do what you wish.

(WERNER *looks at her gloomily and obstinately.*)

FATHER: Wait a moment, Werner. (WERNER *moves away from the Bible with a grunt that could pass for acquiescence.*) What question?

JOHANNA: Why did Franz lock himself up?

FATHER: That's a good many questions in one.

JOHANNA: Tell me what happened.

FATHER (*with light irony*): Well, there was the war.

JOHANNA: Yes, for everybody. Are the others hiding?

FATHER: You don't see those who are hidden.

JOHANNA: He fought, didn't he?

FATHER: Right to the end.

JOHANNA: On what front?

FATHER: In Russia.

JOHANNA: When did he come back?

FATHER: In the autumn of forty-six.

JOHANNA: That's late. Why?

FATHER: His regiment was wiped out. Franz came back on foot all the way through Poland and occupied Germany, hiding as he went. One day the doorbell rang. (*Distant, muffled ring.*) It was he.

(FRANZ *appears upstage, behind his father, in the shadow. He is in civilian clothes, twenty-three or twenty-four years of age.* JOHANNA, WERNER, *and* LENI, *during this flashback scene and the next, do not see the character evoked. Only those who recall him —the* FATHER *in these two memory scenes,* LENI *and the* FATHER *in the third—turn toward those whom they evoke when they speak to them. The voice and actions of the characters who play a memory scene must bear an air of unreality, a faraway quality that, even in the more violent action, distinguishes the past from the present. For the moment, no one sees* FRANZ, *not even the* FATHER.

FRANZ *holds an uncorked bottle of champagne in his right hand. It can be seen only when he takes a drink. A champagne glass placed near him on a console table is hidden by ornaments. He takes it when he wants to drink.*)

JOHANNA: Did he shut himself up right away?

FATHER: Right away in the house; a year later in his room.

JOHANNA: Did you see him every day during that year?

FATHER: Almost every day.

JOHANNA: What did he do?

FATHER: He drank.

JOHANNA: And what did he say?

FRANZ (*in a distant and mechanical voice*): Good morning. Good evening. Yes. No.

JOHANNA: Nothing more?

FATHER: Nothing, except one day. A flood of words. I understood none of it. (*Bitter laugh.*) I was in the library listening to the radio.

(*Crackling of radio, a repeated station call-sign. All these sounds muffled.*)

VOICE FROM THE LOUDSPEAKER: Good evening, listeners. Here is the news. In Nuremberg the International Court sentences Marshal Goering. . . .

(FRANZ *switches off the radio. He remains in shadow even while he moves. The* FATHER *turns with a start.*)

FATHER: What are you doing? (FRANZ *looks at him dully.*) I want to know the sentence.

FRANZ (*his voice cynical and gloomy right through the scene*): To be hanged by the neck until he is dead. (*He drinks.*)

FATHER: How do you know? (FRANZ *is silent.* FATHER *turns to* JOHANNA.) Didn't you read the newspapers at the time?

JOHANNA: Hardly. I was only twelve.

FATHER: They were all in the hands of the Allies. "We are Germans, therefore we are guilty; we are guilty because we are Germans." Every day, on every page. What an obsession! (*To* FRANZ) Eighty million criminals. What a filthy trick! At the most there were three dozen of them. Let them hang those and rehabilitate us. It would be the end of a nightmare. (*With authority*) Will you please turn on the radio. (FRANZ *drinks without moving. Dryly*) You drink too

much. (FRANZ *gazes at him with such a hard expres-*
sion that the FATHER *is silent, abashed. A pause, then*
the FATHER *resumes with an ardent desire to under-*
stand.) What do they gain by reducing a people to
despair? What have I done to merit the contempt of
the universe? My opinions are well known. And you,
Franz, you who fought to the end? (FRANZ *laughs*
coarsely.) Are you a Nazi?

FRANZ: Hell, no!

FATHER: Then you must choose. Either let those who
were responsible be condemned or make the whole
of Germany shoulder their crimes.

FRANZ (*without moving, bursts into a dry, savage*
laugh): Ha! (*Pause.*) It amounts to the same thing.

FATHER: Are you mad?

FRANZ: There are two ways of destroying a people.
Either condemn them en bloc or force them to repudiate the leaders they adopted. The second is the
worse.

FATHER: I repudiate no one, and the Nazis are not my
leaders. I had to put up with them.

FRANZ: You supported them.

FATHER: What the devil did you expect me to do?

FRANZ: Nothing.

FATHER: As for Goering, I am his victim. Take a walk
around our yards. A dozen air raids—not a shed
standing. That's how he protected them.

FRANZ (*brutally*): I *am* Goering. If they hang him,
they hang me.

FATHER: You loathed Goering!

FRANZ: I obeyed.

FATHER: Your military leaders, yes.

FRANZ: Who did they obey? (*Laughs.*) We hated
Hitler, others loved him. What's the difference? You

supplied him with warships, and I with corpses. Tell me, could we have done more if we had worshipped him?

FATHER: Well? Is everyone guilty?

FRANZ: Good God, no! No one. Except the sleeping dogs who accept the judgment of the victors. Fine victors! We know them. They were the same in 1918, with the same hypocritical virtues. What did they do to us then? What did they do to themselves? Don't you tell me! It's the victors who take charge of history. They did so, and gave us Hitler. Judges? Have they never pillaged, massacred, and raped? Was it Goering who dropped the bomb on Hiroshima? If they judge us, who will judge them? They speak of our crimes in order to justify the crime they are quietly preparing—the systematic extermination of the German people. (*He smashes the glass against the table.*) All are innocent before the enemy. All— you, me, Goering, and the others.

FATHER (*shouts*):   Franz! (*The light dims and fades around* FRANZ.) Franz! (*Short pause. He turns slowly to* JOHANNA *and laughs softly.*) I didn't understand a thing. Did you?

JOHANNA: Not a thing. What then?

FATHER: That's all.

JOHANNA: Wasn't it necessary to choose, though— either all innocent or all guilty?

FATHER: He did not choose.

JOHANNA (*thinks a moment, then*): That doesn't make sense.

FATHER: Perhaps it does. . . . I don't know.

LENI (*quickly*): Don't look too far, Johanna. My brother didn't care about Goering and the Air Force, especially as he was in the infantry. For him, there

were guilty and innocent, but they were not the
same. (*To the* FATHER, *who is about to speak*) I
know. I see him every day. The innocent were twenty
years old, they were the soldiers; the guilty were fifty,
they were the fathers.

JOHANNA: I see.

FATHER (*He has lost his relaxed good humor. When he
speaks of* FRANZ, *his voice assumes some passion.*):
You see nothing at all. She is lying.

LENI: Father! You know perfectly well that Franz hates
you.

FATHER (*forcefully, to* JOHANNA): Franz loved me more
than anyone.

LENI: Before the war.

FATHER: Before and after.

LENI: In that case, why do you say: "He loved me"?

FATHER (*taken aback*): Oh, well, Leni . . . we were
talking of the past.

LENI: Don't correct yourself, then. You've given yourself away. (*Pause.*) My brother joined up at eighteen.
If father really wants to tell us why, you will understand the history of this family better.

FATHER: Tell it yourself, Leni. I won't deprive you of
that pleasure.

WERNER (*forcing himself to be calm*): Leni, I warn
you. If you mention a single fact that reflects on my
father, I shall leave this room instantly.

LENI: Are you so afraid of believing me?

WERNER: I won't have my father insulted in my presence.

FATHER (*to* WERNER): Calm down, Werner. I am going to speak. From the beginning of the war the
State gave us orders. We built the Navy. In the
spring of forty-one, the Government gave me to

understand that it wished to purchase a piece of land which we were not using. The land behind the hill —you know it.

LENI: The Government was Himmler. He was looking for a site for a concentration camp. (*Heavy silence.*)

JOHANNA: You knew that?

FATHER (*calmly*): Yes.

JOHANNA: And you agreed?

FATHER (*in the same tone*): Yes. (*Pause.*) Franz discovered the work going on. I had reports that he was always prowling along the barbed wire.

JOHANNA: What happened?

FATHER: Nothing. Silence. It was he who broke it. One day in June, forty-one. (*The* FATHER *turns toward* FRANZ *and looks at him closely while continuing the conversation with* WERNER *and* JOHANNA.) I saw at once that he had put his foot in it. It couldn't have happened at a worse moment. Goebbels and Admiral Doenitz were in Hamburg and were going to visit my new installations.

FRANZ (*youthful voice; soft, affectionate, but worried*): Father, I would like to speak to you.

FATHER (*looking at him*): Have you been down there?

FRANZ: Yes. (*Abruptly and with horror*) Father, they are no longer men.

FATHER: The guards?

FRANZ: The prisoners. I am disgusted with myself, but it is they who fill me with horror. It's their squalor, their vermin, their sores. (*Pause.*) They look as if they are in fear all the time.

FATHER: They are what they have been made.

FRANZ: No one would make me like that.

FATHER: No?

FRANZ: I wouldn't give up.

FATHER: What proof have you that they have given up?

FRANZ: Their eyes.

FATHER: If you were in their place, yours would be the same.

FRANZ: No. (*With a fierce certainty*) No.
(*The* FATHER *looks at him closely.*)

FATHER: Look at me. (*He raises* FRANZ's *chin and looks deep into his eyes.*) Where does it come from?

FRANZ: What?

FATHER: The fear of being a prisoner.

FRANZ: I'm not afraid of it.

FATHER: You want it to happen?

FRANZ: I . . . No.

FATHER: I see. (*Pause.*) You think I shouldn't have sold that land?

FRANZ: If you sold it, it was because you couldn't have done otherwise.

FATHER: But I could.

FRANZ (*stunned*): You could have refused?

FATHER: Certainly. (FRANZ *makes a fierce movement.*) What of it? You no longer trust me.

FRANZ (*consciously mastering himself*): I know that you will explain.

FATHER: What is there to explain? Himmler wanted somewhere to house his prisoners. If I had refused my land, he would have bought some elsewhere.

FRANZ: From others.

FATHER: Exactly. A little farther to the west, a little farther to the east, the same prisoners would suffer under the same guards, and I would have made enemies inside the Government.

FRANZ (*stubbornly*): You shouldn't have got mixed up in this affair.

FATHER: Why not?

FRANZ: Because you are you.

FATHER: And to give you the Pharisee's joy of washing your hands of it, little puritan.

FRANZ: Father, you frighten me. You do not feel the sufferings of others enough.

FATHER: I shall allow myself to feel them when I have the means to put an end to them.

FRANZ: You never will have.

FATHER: Then I shall not feel their suffering. It is a waste of time. Do you suffer for them? Go on with you! (*Pause.*) You do not love your neighbor, Franz, or you would not dare to despise these prisoners.

FRANZ (*hurt*): I do not despise them.

FATHER: You do despise them. Because they are dirty, and because they are afraid. (*He gets up and walks over to* JOHANNA.) He still believed in human dignity.

JOHANNA: Was he wrong?

FATHER: I don't know anything about that. All I can tell you is that the Gerlachs are victims of Luther. That prophet filled us with an insane pride. (*He goes slowly back to his seat and points to* FRANZ.) Franz used to walk across the hills arguing with himself, and once his conscience said yes, you could have cut him into little pieces and you wouldn't have made him change his mind. I was like him when I was young.

JOHANNA (*with irony*): You had a conscience?

FATHER: Yes. I lost it, out of modesty. It is a luxury for princes. Franz could afford it. When one does nothing, one believes oneself responsible for everything. I worked. (*To* FRANZ) What do you want me to say? That Hitler and Himmler are criminals? All right then, I'll say it. (*Laughing*) A strictly personal opinion and of no value to anyone.

FRANZ: Then we are powerless?

FATHER: Yes, if we choose to be powerless. You can do
nothing for mankind if you spend your time condemning it before God. (*Pause.*) Eighty thousand
workers since March. I'm growing. I'm growing. My
shipyards spring up overnight. I have the most
formidable power.

FRANZ: Of course. You work for the Nazis.

FATHER: Because they work for me. They are the
plebeian on the throne. But they are at war to find
us markets, and I am not going to quarrel with them
over a bit of land.

FRANZ (*stubbornly*): You shouldn't have become mixed
up in it.

FATHER: Little prince! Little prince! Do you want to
carry the whole world on your shoulders? The world
is heavy, and you don't know what it's like. Leave it
alone. Take an interest in the firm. Today it's mine;
tomorrow it will be yours. My flesh and blood, my
power, my strength, your future. In twenty years you
will be the master with ships on all the seas, and who
will remember Hitler then? (*Pause.*) You're a
dreamer.

FRANZ: Not as much as you think.

FATHER: Oh? (*He looks at* FRANZ *closely.*) What have
you done? Something wrong?

FRANZ (*proudly*): No.

FATHER: Something good? (*Long pause.*) My God!
(*Pause.*) Well? Is it serious?

FRANZ: Yes.

FATHER: My little prince, don't worry, I'll fix it up.

FRANZ: Not this time.

FATHER: This time like every other time. (*Pause.*)
Well? (*Pause.*) Do you want me to question you?

(*He reflects.*) Does it concern the Nazis? Good. The camp? Good. (*Suddenly clear*) The Pole! (*He gets up and walks about agitatedly. He speaks to* JOHANNA.) He was a Polish rabbi. He had escaped the day before, and the camp commandant had notified us. (*To* FRANZ) Where is he?

FRANZ: In my room. (*Pause.*)

FATHER: Where did you find him?

FRANZ: In the park. He wasn't even hiding. He escaped through sheer madness. Now he is afraid. If they get their hands on him . . .

FATHER: I know. (*Pause.*) If no one has seen him, the matter can be settled. We can get him away by truck to Hamburg. (FRANZ *is tense.*) Has anyone seen him? Well? Who?

FRANZ: Fritz.

FATHER (*to* JOHANNA, *in a conversational tone*): He was our chauffeur, a real Nazi.

FRANZ: He took the car this morning, saying he was going to the garage in Altona. He hasn't come back yet. (*With a glow of pride*) Am I such a dreamer?

FATHER (*smiling*): More than ever. (*In a changed voice*) Why did you put him in your room? To redeem me? (*Silence.*) Answer! It is for me.

FRANZ: It is for us. You and I are one.

FATHER: Yes. (*Pause.*) If Fritz has denounced you . . .

FRANZ (*continues*): They'll come. I know.

FATHER: Go up to Leni's room, and bolt the door. It's an order. I'll settle everything. (FRANZ *looks at him defiantly.*) What is it?

FRANZ: The prisoner . . .

FATHER: I said—everything. The prisoner is under my roof. Go! (FRANZ *disappears. The* FATHER *sits down again.*)

JOHANNA: Did they come?

FATHER: Forty-five minutes later.

(*An* S.S. MAN *appears upstage. Two men behind him, motionless and silent.*)

S.S.: Heil Hitler.

FATHER: Heil. Who are you and what do you want?

S.S.: We have just found your son in his room with an escaped prisoner he has been hiding since last night.

FATHER: In his room? (*To* JOHANNA) Brave boy, he didn't want to lock himself up in Leni's room. He took all the risks. Good. Well?

S.S.: Do you understand?

FATHER: Very well. My son has just committed a serious blunder.

S.S. (*stunned indignation*): A what? (*Pause.*) Stand up when I speak to you.

(*Telephone rings.*)

FATHER (*without rising*): No.

(*He lifts the receiver and, without even asking who the caller is, hands it to the* S.S. MAN, *who snatches it from him.*)

S.S. (*into telephone*): Hello? Oh! (*Clicks his heels.*) Yes. Yes. Yes. Very good, sir. (*He listens and looks at the* FATHER *with amazement.*) Right. Very good, sir. (*Clicks his heels and hangs up.*)

FATHER (*hard and unsmiling*): A blunder, isn't it?

S.S.: That's all.

FATHER: If you have touched a single hair of his head . . .

S.S.: He threw himself at us.

FATHER (*surprised and worried*): My son? (*The* S.S. MAN *nods.*) Did you hit him?

S.S.: No. I swear to you. We got hold of him. . . .

FATHER (*thoughtfully*): He threw himself at you! That's not like him. You must have provoked him. What did you do? (s.s. MAN *is silent.*) The prisoner! (*He stands up.*) Right in front of him? Right in front of my son? (*Cold but terrible anger*) I think you have exceeded your duty. Your name?

s.s. (*piteously*): Hermann Aldrich.

FATHER: Hermann Aldrich! I give you my word that you will remember the twenty-third of June 1941 all your life. Go.

(s.s. MAN *disappears.*)

JOHANNA: Did he remember it?

FATHER (*smiling*): I think so. But his life wasn't very long.

JOHANNA: And Franz?

FATHER: Released at once. On condition that he enlisted. The following winter, he was a lieutenant on the Russian front. (*Pause.*) What's the matter?

JOHANNA: I don't like this story.

FATHER: I am not saying that it's pleasant. (*Pause.*) That was in forty-one.

JOHANNA (*dryly*): Well?

FATHER: It was necessary to survive.

JOHANNA: The Pole didn't survive.

FATHER (*indifferent*): No. That's not my fault.

JOHANNA: I wonder.

WERNER: Johanna!

JOHANNA: You had forty-five minutes. What did you do to save your son?

FATHER: You know perfectly well.

JOHANNA: Goebbels was in Hamburg and you phoned him.

FATHER: Yes.

JOHANNA: You told him that a prisoner had escaped, and you begged him to be indulgent to your son.

FATHER: I also asked him to spare the prisoner's life.

JOHANNA: Of course. (*Pause.*) When you phoned Goebbels . . .

FATHER: Yes?

JOHANNA: You couldn't have been *sure* that the chauffeur had denounced Franz.

FATHER: Go on! He spied on us constantly.

JOHANNA: Yes, but it is possible that he saw nothing and that he had taken the car for quite another reason.

FATHER: That's possible.

JOHANNA: Naturally, you didn't ask him anything.

FATHER: Who?

JOHANNA: This Fritz. (*The* FATHER *shrugs his shoulders.*) Where is he now?

FATHER: In Italy under a wooden cross.
(*Pause.*)

JOHANNA: I see. Well, we shall never get to the bottom of the matter. If it wasn't Fritz who handed over the prisoner, it must have been you.

WERNER (*violently*): I forbid you . . .

FATHER: Don't keep shouting, Werner. (WERNER *is silent.*) You are right, my child. (*Pause.*) When I took up the telephone, I said to myself: a fifty-fifty chance! (*Pause.*)

JOHANNA: A fifty-fifty chance to murder a Jew. (*Pause.*) Has that never kept you awake?

FATHER (*quietly*): Never.

WERNER (*to* FATHER): Father, I support you unreservedly. All lives are valuable. But, if one must choose, I think the life of a son must come first.

JOHANNA (*softly*): We are not concerned with what you think, Werner, but with what Franz must have thought. What did he think, Leni?

LENI (*smiling*): But you know the Von Gerlachs, Johanna.

JOHANNA: He didn't say anything?

LENI: He left without opening his mouth and never wrote to us. (*Pause.*)

JOHANNA (*to* FATHER): You told him that you would settle everything, and he trusted you. As always.

FATHER: I kept my word. I had obtained an assurance that the prisoner would not be punished. Could I have imagined that they would kill him in front of my son?

JOHANNA: That was in forty-one, father. In forty-one it was prudent to imagine anything. (*She approaches the photographs and looks at them. Pause. She continues to look at one of them.*) He was a little puritan, a victim of Luther, who wanted to pay with his blood for the land you sold. (*She turns toward the* FATHER.) You wiped everything out. What remained was only a game for a rich playboy. With the risk of death, to be sure. But for the partner . . . He understood that he could get away with everything because he counted for nothing.

FATHER (*struck by an idea, pointing to her*): There's the wife he should have had.

(WERNER *and* LENI *turn sharply to him.*)

WERNER (*furious*): What?

LENI: Father, what bad taste!

FATHER (*to them*): She understood right off. (*To* JOHANNA) Didn't you? I ought to have compromised for two years in prison. What a blunder! Anything rather than that he should have gone unpunished.

(*Pause. He is lost in thought.* JOHANNA *still looks at the portraits.* WERNER *stands up and, taking her by the shoulders, turns her toward him.*)

JOHANNA (*coldly*): What's the matter?

WERNER: Don't feel sorry for Franz. He wasn't the type to suffer a setback.

JOHANNA: What do you mean?

WERNER (*pointing to the portrait*): Look! Twelve decorations.

JOHANNA: Twelve more setbacks. He ran after death— no luck, death ran quicker than he did. (*To* FATHER) Let's hear the rest. He fought, he came back in forty-six, and then a year later there was the scandal. What was it?

FATHER: One of our Leni's pranks.

LENI (*modestly*): Father is too kind. I furnished the occasion. Nothing more.

FATHER: Some American officers were billeted on us. She used to lead them on and then, when they were well worked up, she would whisper in their ear "I am a Nazi" and call them dirty Jews.

LENI: To damp their ardor. Amusing, eh?

JOHANNA: Very. And did it work?

FATHER: Sometimes. Sometimes they exploded. One of them took it very badly.

LENI (*to* JOHANNA): An American is either a Jew or an anti-Semite, unless he is both at the same time. That one was not a Jew. He was annoyed.

JOHANNA: What happened?

LENI: He tried to rape me. Franz came to my rescue. They rolled on the floor, the American ended up on top. I took a bottle and gave him a terrific blow.

JOHANNA: Did it kill him?

FATHER (*very calm*): What do you think? His skull

broke the bottle. (*Pause.*) Six weeks in the hospital. Naturally, Franz took the blame.

JOHANNA: The blow with the bottle, too?

FATHER: Everything. (*Two American officers appear upstage. The* FATHER *turns toward them.*) It was a mistake, pardon the word, a serious mistake. (*Pause.*) I beg you to thank General Hopkins on my behalf. Tell him my son will leave Germany as soon as he gets his visas.

JOHANNA: For the Argentine?

FATHER (*He turns toward her as the Americans disappear.*): That was the condition.

JOHANNA: I see.

FATHER (*carelessly*): The Americans were really very good.

JOHANNA: Like Goebbels in forty-one.

FATHER: Better! Much better! Washington was counting on re-establishing our enterprise and giving us the job of building up the merchant fleet.

JOHANNA: Poor Franz!

FATHER: What could I do? There were big interests at stake which weighed more heavily than a captain's skull. Even if I had not intervened, the occupying forces would have hushed up the scandal.

JOHANNA: It is quite possible. (*Pause.*) Did he refuse to leave?

FATHER: Not at first. (*Pause.*) I had obtained the visas. He was to have left us on Saturday. On Friday morning Leni came to tell me that he would never come down again. (*Pause.*) At first I thought he was dead. Then I saw my daughter's eyes. She had won.

JOHANNA: Won what?

FATHER: She never said.

LENI (*smiling*): Here, you know, we play loser wins.

JOHANNA: What happened after that?

FATHER: We lived for thirteen years.

JOHANNA (*turns toward the portrait*): Thirteen years.

WERNER: What a nice job! Believe me, as an amateur, I have appreciated everything. How you have twisted her around. To begin with, she hardly listened. In the end, she couldn't stop asking questions. The picture is complete. (*Laughing*) "You are the wife he should have had!" Bravo, Father! That's genius!

JOHANNA: Stop, or we shall be lost!

WERNER: We are lost. What is there left? (*He seizes her arm above the elbow, draws her to him, and looks at her.*) Where are you? You have the eyes of a statue. Blank. (*Pushing her away from him abruptly*) Such common flattery, and you walked right into the trap! You disappoint me, my dear.

(*Pause. They all look at him.*)

JOHANNA: Now is the moment.

WERNER: What?

JOHANNA: To stake everything, my love.

WERNER: Who?

JOHANNA: You. (*Pause.*) They've caught us. When they were talking to me of Franz, they contrived to make their words ricochet to you.

WERNER: Then perhaps it is I who have been taken in?

JOHANNA: No one has. They wanted to make you think I had been taken in.

WERNER: Why, if you please?

JOHANNA: To remind you that nothing belongs to you, not even your wife. (*The* FATHER *softly rubs his hands. Pause. Abruptly*) Take me away from here! (*Short pause.*) I beg you! (WERNER *laughs. She becomes cold and hard.*) For the last time I ask you, let us leave. For the last time, do you hear?

WERNER: I hear. Have you any further questions to ask me?

JOHANNA: No.

WERNER: Then I do as I wish? (JOHANNA *nods, exhausted.*) Very well. (*On the Bible*) I swear to abide by the last wishes of my father.

FATHER: You will stay here?

WERNER (*his hand still on the Bible*): Since you demand it. This house is mine to live in and to die in. (*He lowers his head.*)

FATHER (*rises and goes to him; with affectionate pride*): Well done. (*He smiles at him.* WERNER *frowns an instant, then ends by smiling at him in humble gratitude.*)

JOHANNA (*looking at everyone*): So that's a family conference! (*Pause.*) Werner, I am leaving. With or without you. Choose.

WERNER (*not looking at her*): Without.

JOHANNA: Very well. (*Short pause.*) I hope you will not miss me too much.

LENI: You will miss us. Especially father. When are you leaving us?

JOHANNA: I don't know yet. When I am sure I have lost.

LENI: Aren't you sure?

JOHANNA (*with a smile*): Well, no. Not yet.
(*Pause.*)

LENI (*thinks she understands*): If the police come, all three of us will be arrested for illegal restraint. And, in addition, I shall be charged with murder.

JOHANNA (*unmoved*): Do I look like the sort of person to inform the police? (*To the* FATHER) May I leave?

FATHER: Good night, my child.

(*She bows and goes out.* WERNER *begins to laugh.*)

WERNER (*laughing*): Well, well . . . (*He stops abruptly, approaches his* FATHER, *and touches him timidly on the arm, looking at him with anxious affection.*) Are you pleased?

FATHER (*in horror*): Don't touch me! (*Pause.*) The conference is over. Go and join your wife.

(WERNER *gives him a despairing look, then turns and goes out.*)

LENI: All the same, don't you think you were too hard?

FATHER: With Werner? If it were necessary, I would be soft, but I have found that hardness pays.

LENI: You shouldn't drive him too far.

FATHER: Bah!

LENI: His wife is planning something.

FATHER: Theatrical threats. Resentment brought out the actress, and the actress had to have her exit.

LENI: I hope to God you're right. (*Pause.*) See you this evening, father. (*She waits for him to go out. He does not move.*) I have to close the shutters, and then it will be time for Franz. (*Insistent*) See you this evening.

FATHER (*smiling*): I'm going, I'm going! (*Pause. Somewhat timidly*) Does he know what is wrong with me?

LENI (*astonished*): Who? Oh! Franz! Goodness, no.

FATHER: Ah! (*With painful irony*) You wish to spare him?

LENI: As far as he's concerned, you could throw yourself under a train. (*Indifferently*) To tell you the truth, I forgot to tell him.

FATHER: Make a knot in your handkerchief.

LENI (*taking her handkerchief in order to make a knot*): There!

FATHER: You won't forget?

LENI: No, but I'll have to wait for an opportune moment.

FATHER: When it comes, try also to ask him to see me.

LENI (*wearily*): Again! (*Hard but without anger*) He will not see you. Why force me to repeat every day what you have known for thirteen years?

FATHER (*furiously*): What do I know, you bitch? What do I know? You can't open your mouth without lying. I don't know if you give him my letters and pass on my requests, and I sometimes wonder whether you haven't convinced him that I have been dead for ten years.

LENI (*shrugs her shoulders*): What do you expect to get out of it?

FATHER: I want the truth, or an end to your lies.

LENI (*pointing to the first floor*): The truth is up there. Go up, and you will find it. Go up! Go on!

(*The* FATHER's *anger subsides. He seems frightened.*)

FATHER: You are mad!

LENI: Question him. You will set your mind at rest.

FATHER (*still apprehensive*): I don't even know . . .

LENI: The signal! (*Laughing*) Oh, yes, you know it. I've caught you spying on me a hundred times. I have heard your step and I have seen your shadow. I haven't said anything, but I could hardly keep myself from laughing. (*The* FATHER *tries to protest.*) Am I wrong? Well, I shall have the pleasure of giving it to you myself.

FATHER (*dully and in spite of himself*): No.

LENI: Give four knocks, then five, then three knocks twice. What's holding you back?

FATHER: What should I find? (*Pause. In a dull voice*) I couldn't bear it if he drove me away.

LENI: You'd rather convince yourself that I am pre-
venting his falling into your arms.

FATHER (*painfully*): You must excuse me, Leni. I am
often unjust. (*He strokes her hair; she stiffens.*) Your
hair is soft. (*He caresses her more absent-mindedly,
as if he were thinking.*) Have you any influence over
him?

LENI (*proudly*): Naturally.

FATHER: Couldn't you, little by little, by handling it
cleverly . . . I beg you to stress the main thing—
that my first visit will also be my last. I will only
stay an hour. Less, if that tires him. And, above all,
be sure to tell him that I am not in any hurry.
(*Smiling*) There, that's not too much.

LENI: One meeting only.

FATHER: One only.

LENI: One only, and then you will die. What's the
good of seeing him again?

FATHER: Just to see him again. (*She laughs insolently.*)
And to take leave.

LENI: What difference would it make if you took
French leave?

FATHER: For me? Everything. If I see him again, I close
the account and make out the bill.

LENI: Do you have to take so much trouble? The bill
will be made out in any case.

FATHER: Do you think so? (*Short pause.*) I must draw
it up myself; otherwise, everything will be at loose
ends. (*With a smile that is almost timid*) After all,
I have lived this life; I don't want it to be wasted.
(*Pause. Almost timidly*) Will you speak to him?

LENI (*brutally*): Why should I? After thirteen years of
standing guard, should I relax my vigilance with
only six months to go?

FATHER: Do you stand guard against me?

LENI: Against all those who want to destroy him.

FATHER: I want to destroy Franz?

LENI: Yes.

FATHER (*violently*): Are you mad? (*He calms himself. With a strong desire to convince, almost pleadingly*) Listen, our opinions may differ as to what is best for him. But I am only asking to see him once. How would I have the time to harm him, even if I wanted to? (*She laughs coarsely.*) I give you my word. . . .

LENI: Have I asked you for it? I want none of your gifts!

FATHER: But let's get things clear.

LENI: The Von Gerlachs don't give explanations.

FATHER: You think you've got me, don't you?

LENI (*same voice, same smile*): I have, in a way, haven't I?

FATHER (*ironic grimace, disdainful*): That's what you think!

LENI: Which of us two, father, needs the other?

FATHER (*softly*): Which of us two, Leni, is afraid of the other?

LENI: I am not afraid of you. (*Laughing*) What bluff! (*She looks at him defiantly.*) Do you know what makes me invulnerable? I am happy.

FATHER: You? What can you know of happiness?

LENI: And you? What do you know of it?

FATHER: I see you. If he has given you those eyes, it is the most refined of tortures.

LENI (*almost distraught*): Yes! The most refined! The most refined! I am dizzy! If I stop, I shall crack up. That's happiness, mad happiness. (*Triumphantly and wickedly*) I see Franz! I! I have all I want. (*The FATHER laughs softly. She stops suddenly and stares*

at him.) No. You never bluff. I suppose you have a
trump. All right, show it.

FATHER (*good-humored*): Right away?

LENI (*hardening*): Right away. You are not going to
keep it up your sleeve to bring out when I am not
expecting it.

FATHER (*still good-humored*): And if I don't want to
show it?

LENI: I shall force you to.

FATHER: How?

LENI: I stay put. (*She takes the Bible with an effort
and places it on a table.*) Franz will never see you,
I swear it. (*Placing her hand on the Bible*) I swear
on this Bible that you will die without seeing him
again. (*Pause.*) There. (*Pause.*) Lay down your cards.

FATHER (*calmly*): Well, I never! You didn't have one
of your laughs. (*He strokes her hair.*) When I stroke
your hair, I think of the earth—covered in silk on
top, in a ferment underneath. (*He rubs his hands
softly. With a gentle, inoffensive smile*) I'll leave you,
my child.

(LENI *remains with her eyes fixed on the door upstage
left through which her father has just gone out. She
then pulls herself together, goes to the French
windows on the right, opens them, closes the large
shutters, then closes the glass doors. The room is
plunged in semidarkness. She slowly mounts the
stairs leading to the second floor and knocks at
FRANZ's door—four knocks, then five, then three
knocks twice.*

*Just as she knocks the two series of three, the door,
right, opens and JOHANNA appears noiselessly. She is
spying.*

The noise can be heard of a bolt being drawn and

an iron bar being lifted. The door above is opened, letting out a shaft of electric light from FRANZ'S *room. But he does not appear.* LENI *enters and closes the door. The bolt is fastened and the iron bar lowered.*

JOHANNA *enters the room, approaches a console table, and taps out the two series of three with her index finger as though to commit them to memory. She has obviously not heard the series of five and four. She begins again. At that moment all the lights of the chandelier light up and she starts, stifling a cry. It is the* FATHER *who appears left and who has switched them on.* JOHANNA *protects her eyes with her hand and forearm.)*

FATHER: Who's there? (*She lowers her hand.*) Johanna! (*Going toward her*) I am very sorry. (*He is in the middle of the room.*) In police interrogations they train spotlights on the accused. What must you think of me for shining all this light into your eyes?

JOHANNA: I think you ought to turn it out.

FATHER (*without moving*): And?

JOHANNA: And that you are not the police, but that you intend to subject me to a police interrogation. (*The* FATHER *smiles and lets his hands fall in mock surrender. Quickly*) You never enter this room. What were you doing if you were not spying on me?

FATHER: But you never come here either, my child. (JOHANNA *does not reply.*) The interrogation will not take place. (*He turns on two lamps with rose muslin shades and goes to turn out the chandelier.*) Here we have the rosy light of half-truths. Are you more comfortable?

JOHANNA: No. Do you mind if I go?

FATHER: You may go when you have heard my answer.

JOHANNA: I haven't asked anything.

FATHER: You asked me what I was doing here, and I must tell you even though I have no reason to be proud of it. (*Short pause.*) For years, almost every day when I am sure that Leni will not catch me, I have sat here in this armchair and have waited.

JOHANNA (*interested in spite of herself*): What?

FATHER: In case Franz should walk about in his room and I should be lucky enough to hear him walk. (*Pause.*) That is all they have left me of my son—the sound of his two shoes on the floor. (*Pause.*) At night I get up. Everyone is asleep. I know that Franz is awake. He and I suffer from the same insomnia. It is a way of being together. And you, Johanna, who are you spying on?

JOHANNA: I was not spying on anyone.

FATHER: Then it is a coincidence, a most extraordinary and fortunate coincidence. I was hoping to speak to you alone. (JOHANNA *is irritated. Quickly*) No, no. No secrets, no secrets, except from Leni. You can tell Werner everything, I promise you.

JOHANNA: In that case, the simplest thing would be to call him.

FATHER: I only ask for two minutes. Two minutes and I shall call him myself. If you still want me to.

(*Surprised by his last sentence,* JOHANNA *stops and faces him.*)

JOHANNA: All right. What do you want?

FATHER: To talk to my daughter-in-law about the young Gerlach ménage.

JOHANNA: The young Gerlach ménage is in pieces.

FATHER: What are you saying?

JOHANNA: Nothing new. You've smashed it.

FATHER (*distressed*): Good lord! I must have been

clumsy. (*Solicitously*) But I thought you had a way of patching it up. (*She goes rapidly upstage left.*) What are you doing?

JOHANNA (*turning on all the lights*): The interrogation has begun. I am turning on the spotlights. (*Coming back and standing under the chandelier*) Where should I stand? Here? Good. Now, under the cold light of the whole truths and perfect lies, I declare that I will not make any confessions for the simple reason that I have none to make. I am alone, without strength and completely aware of my powerlessness. I am going to leave. I shall wait for Werner in Hamburg. If he doesn't come back . . . (*She makes a despairing gesture.*)

FATHER (*gravely*): Poor Johanna, we have brought you nothing but misfortune. (*In a changed voice, suddenly confidential and jolly*) And, above all, make yourself beautiful.

JOHANNA: I beg your pardon?

FATHER (*smiling*): I say, make yourself beautiful.

JOHANNA (*almost outraged, violently*): Beautiful!

FATHER: That won't be any trouble.

JOHANNA (*still angry*): Beautiful! The day we say goodbye, I suppose, to leave you with pleasanter memories.

FATHER: No, Johanna. The day you go and see Franz. (JOHANNA *is transfixed.*) The two minutes are up. Shall I call your husband? (*She shakes her head.*) Very well. This will be our secret.

JOHANNA: Werner will know everything.

FATHER: When?

JOHANNA: In a few days. Yes, I'll see him, your Franz, I'll see this domestic tyrant, but it would be better to address yourself to God than to his saints.

FATHER (*after a pause*): I am glad you will try your luck. (*He begins rubbing his hands and then puts them in his pockets.*)

JOHANNA: I'm not so sure about it.

FATHER: Why?

JOHANNA: Because our interests are opposed. I hope that Franz will resume a normal life.

FATHER: I hope so too.

JOHANNA: You? If he puts his nose outside, the police will arrest him and the family will be dishonored.

FATHER (*smiling*): I don't think you realize my power. My son has merely to come down, and I will arrange everything at once.

JOHANNA: That would be the best way to make him run straight up to his room again and lock himself in it forever.

(*Pause. The* FATHER *looks down at the carpet.*)

FATHER (*dully*): A ten-to-one chance that he'll open the door to you, a hundred-to-one that he'll listen to you, and a thousand-to-one that he'll answer you. If you had this thousand-to-one chance . . .

JOHANNA: Well?

FATHER: Would you agree to tell him that I am going to die?

JOHANNA: Hasn't Leni . . . ?

FATHER: No.

(*He raises his head.* JOHANNA *looks straight at him.*)

JOHANNA: So that's how it is? (*She continues looking at him.*) You are not lying. (*Pause.*) A thousand-to-one chance. (*She shudders and pulls herself together immediately.*) Must I also ask him if he will see you?

FATHER (*quickly, frightened*): No, no! Just the announcement, nothing more. The old man is going to die. Without comment. It's a promise!

JOHANNA (*smiling*): Sworn on the Bible.

FATHER: Thank you. (*Her eyes have not left him. Under his breath, as though to explain his conduct, but in a dull voice that seems to be directed only to himself*) I would like to help him. Don't attempt anything today. Leni will be down late. He will no doubt be tired.

JOHANNA: Tomorrow?

FATHER: Yes. In the early afternoon.

JOHANNA: Where shall I find you if I need you?

FATHER: You will not find me. (*Pause.*) I am leaving for Leipzig. (*Pause.*) If you fail . . . (*Gesture.*) I shall be back in a few days. By that time you will either have won or lost.

JOHANNA (*distressed*): You are leaving me alone? (*She pulls herself together.*) Why not? (*Pause.*) Well, I wish you a pleasant journey, and I beg you to wish me nothing.

FATHER: Wait! (*With an apologetic smile, but seriously*) I don't want to upset you, my child, but I repeat, you must make yourself beautiful.

JOHANNA: Again!

FATHER: It's thirteen years since Franz has seen anyone. Not a soul.

JOHANNA (*shrugs*): Except Leni.

FATHER: Leni doesn't count. I wonder if he even sees her. (*Pause.*) He will open the door, and what will happen? What if he is afraid? What if he should bury himself forever in solitude?

JOHANNA: What difference would it make if I were to paint my face?

FATHER (*gently*): He used to love beauty.

JOHANNA: What did he know about it, this son of an industrialist?

FATHER: He will tell you tomorrow.

JOHANNA: Nothing of the kind. (*Pause.*) I am not beautiful. Is that clear?

FATHER: If you aren't, who is?

JOHANNA: No one. There are only ugly women in disguise. I will not disguise myself any more.

FATHER: Even for Werner?

JOHANNA: Not even for Werner. You can have him. (*Pause.*) Do you understand the meaning of words? They made me . . . a beauty. A different one for each film. (*Pause.*) Excuse me, it's a sore point with me. If you touch it, I lose my head.

FATHER: It is I who must apologize, my child.

JOHANNA: Let's drop it. (*Pause.*) You couldn't have known. Or perhaps you did know. It doesn't matter. (*Pause.*) I was pretty, I suppose. . . . They came and told me I was beautiful, and I believed them. Did I know what I was living for? We have to justify our lives. The worst of it is: they were wrong. (*Abruptly*) Ships? Does that justify it?

FATHER: No.

JOHANNA: I thought not. (*Pause.*) Franz will take me as I am. With this dress and this face. Any woman is still good enough for any man.

(*A pause. Above their heads* FRANZ *begins to walk. The steps are irregular, sometimes slow and hesitant, sometimes quick and rhythmic, and sometimes marking time. She looks anxiously at the* FATHER *as if asking: "Is that Franz?"*)

FATHER (*answering her look*): Yes.

JOHANNA: And you remain here whole nights. . . .

FATHER (*pale and tense*): Yes.

JOHANNA: I give up.

FATHER: You think he is mad?

JOHANNA: Raving mad.

FATHER: It is not madness.

JOHANNA (*shrugs*): What is it?

FATHER: Misfortune.

JOHANNA: Who can be more unfortunate than a madman?

FATHER: He is.

JOHANNA (*brutally*): I shall not go and see Franz.

FATHER: Yes, you will. Tomorrow, early in the afternoon. (*Pause.*) It is our only chance—yours, his, and mine.

JOHANNA (*turning toward the staircase. Slowly*): I shall climb those stairs, I shall knock at that door. . . . (*Pause. The footsteps have ceased.*) Very well. I shall make myself beautiful. To protect myself. (*The* FATHER *smiles as he rubs his hands.*)

CURTAIN

ACT II

FRANZ'S *room.*

*On the left in a recess, a door that leads to the land-
ing. It is secured with a bolt and an iron bar.*

*Two doors upstage, one on either side of the bed—
one leading to the bathroom and the other to the
toilet. An enormous bed without sheets or mattress,
but with a blanket folded on the bedsprings. A table
against the wall on the right. One chair.*

*On the left is a jumble of broken furniture and bric-a-
brac. This pile of rubbish is all that remains of the
room's furnishings. On the wall at the back, a large
portrait of Hitler above and to the right of the bed.
Also on the right, some shelves with tape-recorder
spools.*

*Placards on the walls, with texts in printed letters done
by hand:* DON'T DISTURB, FEAR IS FORBIDDEN! *On the
table: oysters, bottles of champagne, champagne
glasses, a ruler, etc. Mildew on the walls and on the
ceiling.* FRANZ *is wearing a tattered uniform, and
his skin shows through the tears. He is seated at the
table, his back turned to* LENI *and three quarters
turned away from the audience. The tape recorder is
hidden under the table.*

LENI *is facing the audience, a white apron over her
dress, sweeping the floor. She is working quietly and
without undue haste like a good housewife, her face
void of expression, almost trancelike, while* FRANZ *is*

speaking. From time to time, however, she glances quickly at him. It is clear that she is watching him and waiting for the speech to end.

FRANZ: Masked inhabitants of the ceilings, your attention, please! Masked inhabitants of the ceilings, your attention, please! They are lying to you. Two thousand million false witnesses! Two thousand million lies a second! Listen to the plea of mankind: "We were betrayed by our deeds. By our words, by our lousy lives!" Decapods, I bear witness that they didn't think what they were saying and that they didn't do what they wished. We plead not guilty. And, above all, don't condemn on the basis of statements, even signed statements. They said at the time: "The accused has made a statement, therefore he is innocent." Dear listeners, my century was a rummage sale in which the liquidation of the human species was decided upon in high places. They began with Germany, and struck right to the bone. (*He pours himself a drink.*) One alone speaks the truth: the shattered Titan, the eyewitness, ageless, regular, secular, *in saecula saeculorum*. Me. Man is dead, and I am his witness. Centuries, I shall tell you how my century tasted, and you will acquit the accused. To hell with the facts; I leave them to the false witnesses. I leave to them the relevant causes and the fundamental reasons. This was how it tasted. Our mouths were full of it. (*He drinks.*) And we drank to get rid of it. (*Dreamily*) It was a queer taste, wasn't it? (*He stands up quickly in a kind of horror.*) I'll come back to it later.

LENI (*thinking that he has finished*): Franz, I have to talk to you.

FRANZ (*shouts*): Silence, in the presence of the Crabs!

LENI (*in a calm voice*): Listen to me! It's serious.

FRANZ (*to the Crabs*): You've chosen to wear shells?
Bravo! Farewell, nakedness! But why have you kept
your eyes? That was the ugliest thing about us. Eh?
Why? (*He pretends to wait. A click. He starts. In a
different voice, dry, quick, and raucous*) What's that?
(*He turns toward* LENI *and looks at her angrily and
defiantly.*)

LENI (*calmly*): The spool. (*She stoops down, picks up
the tape recorder, and places it on the table.*) Finished. . . . (*She presses the button and the spool
rewinds, giving* FRANZ's *speech in reverse.*) Now
you're going to listen to me. (FRANZ *sinks into the
chair, clutching his breast. She stops speaking suddenly and turns to him, seeing him tense and ap-
parently in pain. Without emotion*) What's the
matter?

FRANZ: What do you think?

LENI: Your heart?

FRANZ (*painfully*): It's thumping away.

LENI: What do you want, mastersinger? Another spool?

FRANZ (*suddenly calm*): Certainly not! (*He stands up
and laughs.*) I'm dead. Dead tired, Leni. Take that
away! (*She goes to take off the spool.*) Wait! I want
to hear myself.

LENI: From the beginning?

FRANZ: Anywhere you like. (LENI *starts the machine,
and* FRANZ's *voice is heard: "One alone speaks the
truth," etc.* FRANZ *listens for a moment to his recorded voice, his face tense, then he speaks above
the recorded voice.*) I didn't mean to say that. But
who's speaking? Not a word of truth. (*He listens
again.*) I can't stand that voice any more. It's dead.

For God's sake, stop it! Stop it! You're driving me mad. . . . (LENI, *with no undue haste, stops the machine. She rewinds the spool, takes it off, writes a number on it, and places it on the shelf near the others.* FRANZ *looks at her, downcast.*) Good. I'll have to begin again.

LENI: *As usual.*

FRANZ: Not at all. I'm making progress. One day the words will come by themselves, and I shall say what I want to. Then I'll have some rest. (*Pause.*) Do you think there is such a thing?

LENI: What?

FRANZ: Rest?

LENI: No.

FRANZ: That's what I thought.
(*A short pause.*)

LENI: Will you listen to me?

FRANZ: Eh?

LENI: I'm afraid.

FRANZ (*with a start*): Afraid? (*He looks at her with some concern.*) Did you say afraid?

LENI: Yes.

FRANZ (*brutally*): Then get out!
(*He takes a ruler from the table and taps a placard that reads:* FEAR IS FORBIDDEN!)

LENI: Right. I'm no longer afraid. (*Pause.*) Please listen to me.

FRANZ: That's what I'm doing. You're making my head split. (*Pause.*) Well?

LENI: I don't know exactly what they're planning. . . .

FRANZ: They're planning something? Where? Washington? Moscow?

LENI: Under your very feet.

FRANZ: On the ground floor? (*Suddenly aware.*) Father's going to die.

LENI: Who's talking about father? He'll bury the lot of us.

FRANZ: Good.

LENI: Good?

FRANZ: Good, bad, to hell with it. Well? What's going on?

LENI: You're in danger.

FRANZ (*with conviction*): Yes. After my death. If the centuries lose trace of me, I'll be devoured. And who'll save mankind, Leni?

LENI: Whoever wants to. Franz, your life has been in danger since yesterday.

FRANZ (*indifferently*): Then defend me. That's your job.

LENI: Yes, if you help me.

FRANZ: Haven't the time. (*Peevishly*) I'm writing history, and you come and worry me with your tales.

LENI: It would be a fine tale if they killed you.

FRANZ: Yes.

LENI: If they killed you too soon?

FRANZ (*frowning*): Too soon? (*Pause.*) Who wants to kill me?

LENI: The occupation forces.

FRANZ: I see. (*Pause.*) They silence my voice, and they are confounding the thirtieth century with faked documents. (*Pause.*) Have they someone in the house?

LENI: I think so.

FRANZ: Who?

LENI: I don't know yet. I think it's Werner's wife.

FRANZ: The hunchback?

LENI: Yes. She ferrets about everywhere.

FRANZ: Give her some rat poison.

LENI: She's suspicious.

FRANZ: What a nuisance! (*Worried*) I need ten years.

LENI: Give me ten minutes.

FRANZ: You bore me.

(*He goes to the upstage wall and passes his hand over the spools on the shelf.*)

LENI: Suppose they stole them?

FRANZ (*turning suddenly*): What?

LENI: The spools.

FRANZ: You're losing your head.

LENI (*dryly*): Suppose they came when I wasn't here —or, even better, after they had killed me?

FRANZ: Well? I wouldn't open the door. (*Amused*) Do they want to kill you too?

LENI: They're thinking of doing so. What would you do without me? (FRANZ *does not reply.*) You would die of hunger.

FRANZ: I've no time to be hungry. I shall die, that's all. I speak. Death will take my body, but I won't even notice it. I shall continue to speak. (*Pause.*) One advantage is that you won't blindfold me. My eyes pierce the door, and what do they see? The corpse of murdered Germany. (*Laughing*) I shall stink like a bad conscience.

LENI: They won't pierce anything. They'll knock, you will still be alive, and you will open the door.

FRANZ (*amused surprise*): I?

LENI: You. (*Pause.*) They know the signal.

FRANZ: They can't know it.

LENI: You can be sure they've picked it up since they started spying on me. I'm sure father knows it.

FRANZ: Ah! (*Pause.*) Is he in the plot?

LENI: Who knows? (*Pause.*) I tell you, you will open the door.

FRANZ: What then?

LENI: They'll take the spools.

(FRANZ *opens a drawer of the table, takes out a service revolver, and shows it to* LENI.)

FRANZ (*smiling*): What about that?

LENI: They won't take them by force. They'll persuade you to give them up. (FRANZ *bursts into laughter.*) I beg you, Franz, let's change the signal. (FRANZ *stops laughing. He looks at her in a cunning and hunted way.*) Well?

FRANZ: No. (*He improvises reasons for refusing.*) Everything is in place. History is sacred. If you change a single comma, nothing will be left.

LENI: Splendid. Let's leave history alone. You'll make them a present of your spools, and your tape recorder into the bargain.

(FRANZ *goes up to the spools and looks at them in a hunted way.*)

FRANZ (*at first hesitant and torn with conflict*): The spools . . . the spools . . . (*Pause. He considers a moment, then with a swift gesture of his left hand he sweeps them onto the floor.*) That's what I do with them. (*He speaks in a kind of exultation, as though confiding an important secret to* LENI. *Actually, he is improvising as he goes along.*) It was only a precaution, in case the thirtieth hadn't discovered the window.

LENI: A window? That's something new. You've never mentioned it before.

FRANZ: I don't tell you everything, little sister. (*He rubs his hands happily, like the* FATHER *in Act One.*) Imagine a black window. Finer than ether. Ultrasensitive. It records the slightest breath. The *slightest* breath. All history is engraved on it, from the beginning of time up to this snap of my fingers. (*He snaps his fingers.*)

LENI: Where is it?

FRANZ: The window? Everywhere. Here. It's the day in reverse. They will invent machines to make it vibrate, and everything will come back to life. You see? (*In a sudden transport*) All our actions. (*He resumes his savage and inspired tone.*) Like a film, I tell you. The Crabs sitting round watching Rome burn and Nero dance. (*To the photo of Hitler*) They'll see you, little father. For you danced, didn't you? (*He kicks the spools.*) Burn them! Burn them! What the hell do I want with them? Take them away! (*Suddenly*) What were you doing on the sixth of December 1944 at eight thirty p.m.? (LENI *shrugs her shoulders.*) You don't remember? They know. They've got your whole life spread out, Leni. I'm discovering the horrible truth. We're under observation all the time.

LENI: We are?

FRANZ (*facing out front*): You, me, all the dead, mankind. (*He laughs.*) Be on your guard. They're watching you. (*Darkly, to himself*) No one is alone. (LENI *gives a short laugh.*) Laugh while you can, my poor Leni, the thirtieth will arrive like a thief in the night; the turn of a handle, the vibrating night. You'll land in the middle of them.

LENI: Living?

FRANZ: A thousand years dead.

LENI (*with indifference*): Bah!

FRANZ: Dead and revived. The window will reveal everything, even our thoughts. See? (*Pause. With an*

anxiety that may or may not be sincere) What if
we are already there?

LENI: Where?

FRANZ: In the thirtieth century. Are you sure this
comedy is being played for the first time? Are we
living, or reincarnated? (*He laughs.*) Be on your
guard! If the Decapods are watching us, you may be
sure they find us very ugly.

LENI: How do you know?

FRANZ: Crabs only like Crabs. It's only natural.

LENI: Suppose they are men?

FRANZ: In the thirtieth century? If there is a man left,
he'll be preserved in a museum. . . . Do you think
they'll still have our nervous system?

LENI: And will Crabs do that?

FRANZ (*curtly*): Yes. (*Pause.*) They'll have different
bodies and, therefore, different ideas. What ideas, eh?
What? Can you grasp the importance of my task
and its exceptional difficulty? I am defending you
before judges whom I haven't the pleasure of knowing. Working blind. You drop a word here to the
judge, and it tumbles down the centuries. What will
it mean up there? Do you know I sometimes say
white when I mean to say black? (*He suddenly
slumps into his chair.*) Good God!

LENI: Now what?

FRANZ (*overcome*): The window!

LENI: Well?

FRANZ: It's all direct transmission now. We have to be
on our guard all the time. It was a good thing I found
out about it. (*Savagely*) Explain! Justify! Not a
moment's respite. Men, women, hunted executioners,
relentless victims, I am your martyr.

LENI: If they see everything, why do they need your commentaries?

FRANZ (*laughing*): Ha! But they are Crabs, Leni. They don't understand anything. (*He wipes his brow with his handkerchief, looks at the handkerchief, and throws it in disgust onto the table.*) Salt water!

LENI. What did you expect?

FRANZ (*shrugging his shoulders*): Blood. I've earned it. (*He stands up, alert and with false gaiety.*) Follow my orders, Leni. I'll get you to speak directly to them. A test for voice. Speak loudly and pronounce clearly. (*Very loud*) Testify before the judges that the crusaders of democracy don't want to let us rebuild the walls of our houses. (LENI, *annoyed, remains silent.*) Go on. If you obey me, I'll listen to you.

LENI (*to the ceiling*): I declare that everything is in ruins.

FRANZ: Louder!

LENI: Everything is in ruins.

FRANZ: What's left of Munich?

LENI: A few bricks.

FRANZ: Hamburg.

LENI: A no man's land.

FRANZ: Where are the last Germans?

LENI: In the cellars.

FRANZ (*to the ceiling*): Well, do you grasp that? After thirteen years! Grass covers the streets; our machines are tangled among the weeds. (*Pretending to listen*) A punishment? What a filthy lie! No competition in Europe—that's the principle and the doctrine. Say what's left of the firm.

LENI: Two slipways.

FRANZ: Two! Before the war we had a hundred! (*He rubs his hands, and speaks to* LENI *in his natural voice.*) Enough for today. Your voice is weak, but it would do if you let it go. (*Pause.*) Now speak! Well? (*Pause.*) So they want to sap my morale?

LENI: Yes.

FRANZ: A bad move. My morale is like steel.

LENI: My poor Franz! He'll do as he likes with you.

FRANZ: Who?

LENI: The representative of the occupation forces.

FRANZ: Ha! Ha!

LENI: He'll knock, you'll open up, and do you know what he'll say?

FRANZ: I don't give a damn!

LENI: He'll say: "you imagine you're the witness, but you're the accused." (*Short pause.*) What will you reply?

FRANZ: Get out! You're in their pay. You're the one who's trying to demoralize me.

LENI: What will you reply, Franz? What will you reply, Franz? What will you reply? For twelve years now you've been prostrating yourself before this tribunal of the future, and you have conceded it every right. Why not the right to condemn you?

FRANZ (*shouting*): Because I'm a witness for the defense.

LENI: Who appointed you?

FRANZ: History.

LENI: It has happened, hasn't it, that a man believed himself appointed by history, only to find it was someone else?

FRANZ: That won't happen to me. You'll all be acquitted. Even you. That'll be my revenge. I'll put history into a mousehole. (*He stops, worried.*) Ssh! They're listening. You egg me on; you egg me on until I forget myself. (*To the ceiling*) I beg your pardon, listeners; my words have betrayed my thoughts.

LENI (*savage and ironic*): There he is—the man with morale like steel! (*Contemptuously*) You spend your time begging pardon.

FRANZ: I'd like to see you in my place. They're going to grind tonight.

LENI: Do the Crabs grind, then?

FRANZ: They do, up there. It's very unpleasant. (*To the ceiling*) Please take note of my correction, listeners—

LENI (*bursting out*): Stop it! Stop it! Get rid of them.

FRANZ: Are you out of your mind?

LENI: Challenge their competence, I beg you; it's your only weakness. Tell them "You are not my judges," and you'll have no one to fear—either in this world or the next.

FRANZ (*angrily*): Get out!

(*He takes two oyster shells and rubs them together.*)

LENI: I haven't finished clearing up.

FRANZ: Very well. I'm going to the thirtieth. (*He stands up, still keeping his back to her, and goes over to a placard that reads:* DON'T DISTURB. *He turns it around, so that it reads* BACK AT 12 O'CLOCK. *He sits down again and rubs the shells together.*) You're looking at me. I can feel my neck burning. I forbid you to look at me! If you stay, keep working. (LENI *does not move.*) Will you take your eyes off me!

LENI: I will if you speak to me.

FRANZ: You're driving me mad! Mad! Mad!

LENI (*with a mirthless laugh*): You'd like me to.

FRANZ: You want to look at me? Then do so! (*He stands up and does the goose step.*) Left, right, left, right!

LENI: Stop!

FRANZ: Left, right, left, right!

LENI: Please, stop!

FRANZ: What's the matter, my pretty? Afraid of a soldier?

LENI: I'm afraid of despising you.

(*She takes off her apron, throws it on the bed, and goes toward the door.* FRANZ *stops abruptly.*)

FRANZ: Leni! (*She is at the door. He speaks with a rather bewildered gentleness.*) Don't leave me alone!

LENI (*turns, speaking passionately*): Do you want me to stay?

FRANZ (*in the same gentle voice*): I need you, Leni.

LENI (*goes toward him, overcome*): My dear!

(*She is close to him. She raises her hand hesitantly and caresses his face. He allows her to do so for a moment, then jumps back.*)

FRANZ: Keep your distance! Keep a respectful distance! And no emotion.

LENI (*smiling*): Puritan!

FRANZ: Puritan? (*Pause.*) You think so? (*He comes close to her and caresses her shoulders and neck. Though ill at ease, she allows him to do so.*) Puritans don't know how to caress. (*He caresses her breasts. She shudders and closes her eyes.*) But I do. (*She lets herself go against him. He suddenly breaks free.*) Get away! You disgust me!

LENI (*with icy calm, taking a step backward*): Not always!

FRANZ: Always! Always! From the very first day!

LENI: Down on your knees! Why aren't you begging their pardon?

FRANZ: Pardon for what? Nothing has happened!

LENI: What about yesterday?

FRANZ: Nothing, I tell you! Nothing at all!

LENI: Nothing except incest.

FRANZ: You always exaggerate.

LENI: Aren't you my brother?

FRANZ: Yes, of course.

LENI: Haven't you slept with me?

FRANZ: Not very often.

LENI: Even if you did it only once . . . Are you so afraid of words?

FRANZ (*shrugging his shoulders*) Words! (*Pause.*) If we had to find words for all the tribulations of this rotting flesh! (*He laughs.*) Are you trying to say that I make love? Oh, little sister! You are there, and I clasp you. A creature sleeps with its own kind, as it does a thousand million times every night upon this earth. (*To the ceiling*) But I swear to you that Franz, the eldest son of the Gerlachs, has never desired his younger sister, Leni.

LENI: Coward! (*To the ceiling*) Masked inhabitants of the ceiling, the witness of the centuries is a false witness. I, Leni, incestuous sister, love Franz, and I love him because he is my brother. No matter how little you care for family ties, you will condemn us outright, but I couldn't care less. (*To* FRANZ) That's the way to talk to them, you poor lost sheep. (*To the Crabs*) He desires me, but he doesn't love me. He dies of shame, and he sleeps with me in the dark . . . So? I win. I wanted to have him, and I have him.

FRANZ (*to the Crabs*): She's mad. (*He winks at them.*) I'll explain to you when we're alone.

LENI: I forbid you! I shall die; I am already dead, and I forbid you to plead my cause. I have only one judge —myself—and I acquit myself. Oh, witness for the defense, testify before yourself. You will be invulner-

able if you dare to state: "I have done what I wanted,
and I want what I have done."

(FRANZ's *face seems suddenly petrified. He appears
cold, threatening, and filled with hatred.*)

FRANZ (*harshly and defiantly*): What have I done,
Leni?

LENI (*crying out*): Franz! They'll kill you if you don't
defend yourself.

FRANZ: Leni, what have I done?

LENI (*worried, giving ground*): Well . . . I've already
told you.

FRANZ: Incest? No, Leni, it wasn't the incest you were
talking about. (*Pause.*) What have I done?

(*A long silence. They look at each other.* LENI *turns
away first.*)

LENI: All right; I've lost. Forget it. I'll protect you
without your help. I'm used to it.

FRANZ: Get out! (*Pause.*) If you don't obey, I'll go on
a silence strike. You know I can hold out for two
months.

LENI: I know. (*Pause.*) I can't. (*She goes to the door,
lifts the bar, and draws the bolt.*) I'll bring your
dinner this evening.

FRANZ: No use. I won't open the door.

LENI: That's your business. Mine is to bring your
dinner. (*He does not reply. Going out, she speaks to
the Crabs.*) In case he doesn't open the door, good
night, my pretty ones!

(*She goes out and closes the door.* FRANZ *turns, waits
a moment, then lowers the bar and draws the bolt, his
face set. He relaxes as soon as he feels safe and appears reassured and almost gay, but it is now that he
seems most mad. During the following speech he*

speaks to the Crabs. It is not a monologue, but a dialogue carried on with invisible persons.)

FRANZ: Doubtful witness. To be examined in my presence and according to my instructions. (*Pause. Reassured, weary, very softly*) Eh? Tiresome? In a way, yes, rather tiresome. But what a fuss! (*He yawns.*) Her main job is to keep me awake. It has been midnight for twenty years this century. It's not very easy to keep your eyes open at midnight. No, no; just dozing, that's all. It comes over me when I'm alone. (*He becomes increasingly sleepy.*) I shouldn't have sent her away. (*He sways, then quickly straightens up and marches in military style to the table. He bombards the portrait of Hitler with oystershells, shouting*) Sieg! Heil! Sieg! Heil! Sieg! (*He stands at attention and clicks his heels.*) Führer, I am a soldier. If I fall asleep, it's serious, very serious. Abandoning my post. I swear to remain awake. Put on the searchlights, you! Full in my face, right in the eyes. That wakes you up. (*He waits.*) You lousy scum! (*He goes to his chair and speaks in a soft, conciliatory voice.*) Well, I'll sit down awhile. . . . (*He sits down, his head nodding, his eyes blinking.*) Roses . . . Oh, isn't it lovely . . . (*He jumps up so quickly that he knocks over the chair.*) Roses? And if I take the bouquet, they will make me the highlight of their carnival. (*To the Crabs*) A brazen carnival! Help me, friends! I know too much; they want to get me out of the way. That's the great temptation. (*He goes to the bedside table, takes some pills from a bottle, and chews them.*) Ugh! Listeners, take note of my new call-sign, *De profundis clamavi*, D. P. C. Listen, everyone! Grind! Grind away! If you don't listen to me, I'll fall asleep. (*He pours himself some champagne, drinks, spills half of it over his uniform, then lets his hand fall to his side, the glass hanging from his fingers.*) Meanwhile the century gallops on. . . . They've put cotton in my head. Fog—it's white. (*His eyes blink.*) It's spreading over the fields . . . giving them cover. They're creeping up. There'll be bloodshed tonight.

(*The sound of distant shots, noises, galloping. He dozes off.* SERGEANT MAJOR HERMANN *opens the door of the toilet and comes toward* FRANZ, *who is facing the audience with his eyes closed.* HERMANN *salutes, then stands at attention.*)

FRANZ (*in a thick, dull voice, without opening his eyes*): Partisans?

SERGEANT MAJOR: About twenty.

FRANZ: Anyone killed?

SERGEANT MAJOR: No. Two wounded.

FRANZ: Ours?

SERGEANT MAJOR: Theirs. We put them in the barn.

FRANZ: You know my orders. Dismissed!

(*The* SERGEANT MAJOR *looks at* FRANZ, *hesitant, but angry.*)

SERGEANT MAJOR: Very good, lieutenant.

(*Salute. About face. He goes out through the toilet door, closing it behind him. Pause.* FRANZ's *head falls onto his chest. He utters a terrible cry and wakes with a start, facing the audience.*)

FRANZ: No! Heinrich! Heinrich! I said no! (*He rises painfully, takes a ruler from the table, and strikes himself on the fingers of his left hand as though hammering in a lesson.*) Of course I did! (*More blows with the ruler.*) I take full responsibility. What was it she said? (*Taking up* LENI's *words in his own terms*) I do what I like, and I like what I do.

(*Harried.*) Hearing of May 20, 3059, Franz von Gerlach, lieutenant. Don't throw my century into the
ashcan. Not without hearing me. Evil, your lord-
ships, evil was the only material we had. We worked
on it in our refineries, and the finished product became good. Result: the good turned bad. And don't
run away with the idea that the evil turned out well.
(*He smiles, debonair; his head droops.*) Eh?
(*Shouts.*) Falling asleep? Come on! Senile decay.
They want to get at my head. Take care, you judges;
if I rot, my century will be engulfed. The flock of
the centuries needs a black sheep. What will the
fortieth say, Arthropods, if the twentieth has wan-
dered from the fold? (*Pause.*) No help? Never? Thy
will be done. (*He returns to the front of the stage
and goes to sit down.*) Ah! I should never have let
her go. (*Sound of knocking at the door. He listens,
and straightens up. It is the agreed signal. He cries
out joyfully*) Leni! (*He runs to the door, raises the
bar, and draws the bolt with strong and decisive
movements. He is suddenly wide-awake. Speaking as
he opens the door*) Come in quickly! (*He takes a
step back to allow her to pass.* JOHANNA *appears in
the doorway, looking very beautiful, made up and
wearing a long dress.* FRANZ *takes a step backward.*)
FRANZ (*a hoarse cry*): Ha! (*He draws back.*) What's
this? (*She is about to reply, but he stops her.*) Not a
word! (*He retreats and sits down. Sitting astride his
chair, he looks at her, fascinated. He nods agreement
and speaks with a restrained voice*) Yes. (*Brief
pause.*) She will come in . . . (*As he says this, she
comes in.*) . . . and I shall still be alone. (*To the
Crabs*) Thank you, comrades, I needed your help.

(*In a kind of trance*) She will say nothing, and it will be only a vision. I shall look at her.

(JOHANNA *has appeared to be fascinated by him. She recovers, then smiles as she speaks in order to overcome her fear.*)

JOHANNA: Nevertheless, I have to talk to you.

FRANZ (*retreating from her slowly, without taking his eyes off her*): No! (*He strikes the table.*) I knew she would spoil everything. (*Pause.*) It's *someone* now. In my room. Get out! (*She does not move.*) I'll have you thrown out like a tramp.

JOHANNA: By whom?

FRANZ (*shouting*): Leni! (*Pause.*) You're a shrewd one, you've found the weak spot: I'm alone. (*He turns around suddenly. Pause.*) Who are you?

JOHANNA: Werner's wife.

FRANZ: Werner's wife? (*He stands up and looks at her.*) Werner's wife? (*He looks at her in amazement.*) Who sent you?

JOHANNA: No one.

FRANZ: How did you know the signal?

JOHANNA: From Leni.

FRANZ (*with a short laugh*): From Leni! I can well believe that!

JOHANNA: She was knocking. I . . . surprised her at it and counted the knocks.

FRANZ: I was warned that you have your nose in everything. (*Pause.*) Well, madame, you have risked killing me. (*She laughs.*) Laugh! Laugh! I could have had a seizure. What would you have done? I've been ordered not to have visitors—because of my heart. It's liable to lose courage without any warning. As luck would have it, you are beautiful. Oh! One moment. It's over now. I took you for God knows what . . . perhaps a vision. Take advantage of that salutary error to disappear before you commit a crime.

JOHANNA: No.

FRANZ (*shouts*): I'm going to . . . (*He goes toward her threateningly, then stops. He slumps into his chair and feels his heart.*) A hundred and forty at least. For Christ's sake, beat it. Can't you see I'm going to croak any moment?

JOHANNA: That would be the best solution.

FRANZ: What? (*He takes his hand from his chest and looks at* JOHANNA *in surprise.*) She was right. You're in their pay! (*He stands up and walks easily.*) They won't get me so quickly. Take it easy! (*He turns quickly back to her.*) The best solution? For whom? For all the false witnesses of this earth?

JOHANNA: For Werner and me. (*She looks at him.*)

FRANZ (*dumfounded*): Am I in your way?

JOHANNA: You tyrannize us.

FRANZ: I don't even know you.

JOHANNA: You know Werner.

FRANZ: I have even forgotten what he looks like.

JOHANNA: They are keeping us here by force. Because of you.

FRANZ: Who?

JOHANNA: Father and Leni.

FRANZ (*amused*): Do they beat you? Do they chain you up?

JOHANNA: Oh, no.

FRANZ: Well?

JOHANNA: Blackmail.

FRANZ: That, yes. That is like them. (*Dry laugh. His astonishment returns.*) Because of me? What do they want?

JOHANNA: To keep us in reserve. We will take over in case of accident.

FRANZ (*gaily*): Your husband will make my soup and you will sweep out my room? Do you know how to darn?

JOHANNA (*pointing to his ragged uniform*): The needlework will not be very interesting.

FRANZ: Don't fool yourself! These holes are consolidated. If it weren't that my sister has magic fingers . . . (*Suddenly serious*) No changes. Take Werner to the devil, and don't let me see you any more! (*He goes to his chair. Just as he is about to sit, he turns.*) Still there?

JOHANNA: Yes.

FRANZ: You didn't understand me. I give you your freedom.

JOHANNA: You give me nothing at all.

FRANZ: I tell you, you are free.

JOHANNA: Words! Hot air!

FRANZ: You want deeds?

JOHANNA: Yes.

FRANZ. Well, what shall I do?

JOHANNA: The best thing would be to do away with yourself.

FRANZ: Again! (*Laughs shortly.*) Don't count on it. Out of the question.

JOHANNA: (*Pause.*) Then help us.

FRANZ (*choked*): Eh?

JOHANNA (*with warmth*): You must help us, Franz! (*Pause.*)

FRANZ: No. (*Pause.*) I don't belong to this century. I will save the world as a whole, but I will not help anyone in particular. (*He paces agitatedly.*) I forbid you to draw me into your affairs. I am ill, do you understand? They take advantage of it to force me to live in the most abject dependence, and you ought to be ashamed, you who are young and healthy, to ask someone who is weak and oppressed to help you. (*Pause.*) I am delicate, madame, and my peace of mind comes before everything. Doctor's orders. You could be strangled before my very eyes, and I would not lift a finger. (*Complacently*) Do I disgust you?

JOHANNA: Intensely.

FRANZ (*rubbing his hands*): Very good!

JOHANNA: But not enough to make me go.

FRANZ: Good. (*He takes the revolver and aims it at her.*) I shall count three. (*She smiles.*) One! (*Pause.*) Two! (*Pause.*) Phut! No one here. Vanished! (*To the Crabs*) What calm! She is quiet. It's all there, comrades: "Be beautiful and keep quiet!" A vision. Is it inscribed on your window? Oh, no! What could be inscribed on it? Nothing has changed; nothing has happened. The trick brought nothing into the room, that's all. Emptiness, a diamond that cuts no glass, an absence, beauty. You'll see nothing but the blaze there, poor Crustaceans. You took our eyes to examine what exists, while we, living in man's epoch, have seen with those same eyes what does not exist.

JOHANNA (*quietly*): Father is going to die.

(*Pause.* FRANZ *throws the revolver on the table and gets up quickly.*)

FRANZ: Not a chance! Leni has just told me that he is as strong as an oak.

JOHANNA: She lies.

FRANZ (*with assurance*): To everybody except me. It's the rule of the game. (*Quickly*) Go and hide yourself; you ought to die of shame. A ruse so vulgar and so quickly exposed! Eh? Two wonderful opportunities in less than an hour, and you cannot even take advantage of such unheard-of luck! You are a common type, my young sister-in-law, and I am no longer surprised that Werner married you.

(*He turns his back on her, sits down, and knocks two shells against each other. His face gloomy and withdrawn, he ignores* JOHANNA.)

JOHANNA (*disconcerted for the first time*): Franz! (*Silence*) He will die in six months! (*Silence. Overcoming her fear, she approaches him and touches him on the shoulder. No reaction. Her hand falls back. She looks at him for a moment in silence.*) You are right, I did not know how to take advantage of my luck. Goodbye! (*She is about to leave.*)

FRANZ (*quickly*): Wait! (*She turns slowly. He still has his back to her.*) The tablets, over there in the tube. On the bedside table. Hand them to me!

(JOHANNA *goes to the bedside table.*)

JOHANNA: Benzedrine, is that it? (*He nods. She throws the tube to him, and he catches it in flight.*) Why are you taking benzedrine?

FRANZ: To put up with you. (*He swallows four tablets.*)

JOHANNA: Four at a time?

FRANZ: And four more in a little while, which makes eight. (*He drinks.*) They have designs on my life, madame; I know it. You are the tool of a murderer. This is the moment to think clearly, eh? And to the point? (*He takes another tablet.*) There were mists . . . (*Finger on his forehead*) . . . there. I'm letting some sunshine in. (*He drinks, makes a violent effort to control himself, and turns around, his face hard and set.*) This dress, these jewels, these gold chains —who advised you to put them on? To put them on *today*? Father sent you.

JOHANNA: No.

FRANZ: But he gave you his advice. (*She tries to speak.*) Useless! I know him just as if I had made him. To tell you the truth, I am no longer sure which of us made the other. When I want to know what trick he is up to, I begin by emptying my brain, and it always works. The first thoughts that are born are his. Do you know why? He created me in his image —unless he has become the image of what he created. (*He laughs.*) You don't understand? (*Sweeping everything away with a tired gesture*) Tricks with a mirror. (*Imitating his* FATHER) "And be sure to make yourself beautiful!" I can hear it from here. He loves beauty, the old fool; therefore he knows that I set it above everything. Except my own madness. Are you his mistress? (*She shakes her head.*) He must have aged! His accomplice, then?

JOHANNA: Until now I was his enemy.

FRANZ: Switching sides? He loves that. (*Abruptly serious*) Six months?

JOHANNA: Not more.

FRANZ: The heart?

JOHANNA: The throat.

FRANZ: Cancer? (JOHANNA *nods.*) Thirty cigars a day! The idiot! (*Pause.*) Cancer? Then he will kill himself. (*Pause. He gets up, takes some shells, and bombards the portrait of Hitler.*) He will kill himself, the old Führer, he will kill himself! (*Silence.* JOHANNA *looks at him.*) What's the matter?

JOHANNA: Nothing. (*Pause.*) You love him.

FRANZ: As much as I do myself and less than cholera. What does he want? To see me?

JOHANNA: No.

FRANZ: It's just as well he doesn't. (*Shouting*) He can live or die, for all I care! Look what he has made of me! (*He takes the bottle of pills and begins to unscrew the cap.*)

JOHANNA (*gently*): Give me that tube.

FRANZ: Why are you meddling?

JOHANNA (*holding out her hand*): Give it to me!

FRANZ: I have to dope myself. I hate having my habits changed. (*She still holds out her hand.*) I'll give it to you, but you're not to mention this stupid business any more. Agreed? (JOHANNA *makes a vague sign that could pass for a nod of agreement.*) Good. (*He gives her the bottle.*) As for me, I am going to forget the whole thing. At once. I forget what I want to forget. An asset, eh? (*Pause.*) There, *Requiescat in pace.* (*Pause.*) Well? Talk to me!

JOHANNA: About whom? About what?

FRANZ: About anything, except the family. About yourself.

JOHANNA: There is nothing to tell.

FRANZ: That's for me to decide. (*He looks at her closely.*) A trap, that's what you are. (*He runs his eyes over her.*) It's so good, it's professional. (*Pause.*) Actress?

JOHANNA: I was.

FRANZ: And then?

JOHANNA: I married Werner.

FRANZ: You didn't succeed?

JOHANNA: Not enough

FRANZ: An extra? Starlet?

JOHANNA (*with a gesture that denies the past*): Bah!

FRANZ: Star?

JOHANNA: If you like.

FRANZ (*ironic admiration*): Star! And you didn't succeed? What did you want?

JOHANNA: What does one want? Everything.

FRANZ (*slowly*): Everything, yes. Nothing else. All or nothing. (*Laughing*) Turned out badly, eh?

JOHANNA: Always does.

FRANZ: And Werner? Does he want *everything*?

JOHANNA: No.

FRANZ: Why did you marry him?

JOHANNA: Because I loved him.

FRANZ (*gently*): You didn't.

JOHANNA (*bristling*): What?

FRANZ: Those who want everything . . .

JOHANNA (*still bristling*): Well?

FRANZ: . . . can't love.

JOHANNA: I don't want anything now.

FRANZ: Except his happiness, I hope!

JOHANNA: Except that. (*Pause.*) Help us!

FRANZ: What do you expect me to do?

JOHANNA: Come back to life.

FRANZ: Well, I'll be damned! (*Laughing*) You are proposing my suicide.

JOHANNA: It's one or the other.

FRANZ (*with a sneering laugh*): It's all becoming clear! (*Pause.*) I am charged with murder, and it was the announcement of my death which put an end to the proceedings. You knew that, didn't you?

JOHANNA: I knew it.

FRANZ: And you want me to come back to life?

JOHANNA: Yes.

FRANZ: I see. (*Pause.*) If the brother-in-law can't be

killed, then he must be put into safe custody. (*She shrugs her shoulders.*) Must I wait here for the police, or should I give myself up?

JOHANNA (*on edge*): You will not go to prison.

FRANZ: No?

JOHANNA: Of course not.

FRANZ: Then it's because he'll fix it up for me. (JOHANNA *nods.*) He hasn't given up, then? (*With an irony full of resentment*) What hasn't he done for me, the good man! (*Gesture indicating the room and himself*) And look at the result. (*Fiercely*) You can all go to the devil!

JOHANNA (*overwhelmed with disappointment*): Oh, Franz! You're a coward!

FRANZ (*bridling*): What? (*He recovers himself and speaks with deliberate cynicism.*) Yes, I am. So what?

JOHANNA: What about those? (*She flicks his medals with her fingers.*)

FRANZ: Those? (*He takes off a medal and removes its silver-paper wrapping. It is made of chocolate. He eats it.*) Oh, I won them all. They're all mine, so I have the right to eat them. Heroism is my business. But heroes . . . Do you know what they are?

JOHANNA: No.

FRANZ: Well, there are all kinds. Policemen and thieves, soldiers and civilians—not many civilians—cowards and even brave men—the whole caboodle. They have one thing in common—medals. I'm a cowardly hero, and I wear chocolate medals. It's more decent. Do you want one? Don't be shy; I've got over a hundred in my drawer.

JOHANNA: Thank you.

(*He tears off a medal and gives it to her. She eats it.*)

FRANZ (*Suddenly, with violence*): No!

JOHANNA: I beg your pardon?

FRANZ: I won't allow myself to be judged by the wife of my younger brother. (*Emphatically*) I'm not a coward, madame, and I'm not afraid of prison. I live in one. You couldn't stand three days of the life that I have to endure.

JOHANNA: What does that prove? It's of your own choosing.

FRANZ: Mine? But I never choose, my dear girl! I am chosen. Nine months before my birth they had chosen my name, my career, my character, and my fate. I tell you that this prison routine has been forced upon me, and you should understand that I would not submit myself to it unless it was vitally necessary.

JOHANNA: Why is it so vital?

(FRANZ *steps back a pace. Short silence.*)

FRANZ: Your eyes are shining. No, madame, I shall make no confessions.

JOHANNA: You are cornered, Franz. Either your reasons are valid or your younger brother's wife will judge you without mercy. (*She comes up to him, intending to pull off a medal.*)

FRANZ: Are you death? No, take a cross. They're made of Swiss chocolate.

JOHANNA (*taking a cross*): Thanks. (*She draws slightly away from him.*) Death? Do I look like it?

FRANZ: At times.

JOHANNA (*glancing into the mirror*): You amaze me. When?

FRANZ: When you are beautiful. (*Pause.*) They're using you, madame. You're a tool in their hands to get me to talk, and if I tell you anything, I risk

my neck. (*Pause.*) I don't care. I'll risk everything.
Carry on!

JOHANNA (*after a pause*): Why are you hiding here?

FRANZ: First of all, I'm not hiding. If I had wanted to
escape prosecution, I would have gone to Argentina
long ago. (*Pointing to the wall*) There was a window.
Here. It overlooked what was our park.

JOHANNA: *Was?*

FRANZ: Yes. (*They look at each other for a moment.*)
I had it walled up. (*Pause.*) Something is happening.
Outside. Something I don't want to see.

JOHANNA: What?

FRANZ (*looking at her challengingly*): The murder of
Germany. (*He is still looking at her, half pleadingly,
half threateningly, as though to keep her from speaking. They have reached the danger point.*) Be quiet!
I've seen the ruins.

JOHANNA: When?

FRANZ: Coming back from Russia.

JOHANNA: That was fourteen years ago.

FRANZ: Yes.

JOHANNA: And you believe nothing has changed?

FRANZ: I *know* that everything is getting worse every
hour.

JOHANNA: Is it Leni who tells you?

FRANZ: Yes.

JOHANNA: Do you read the papers?

FRANZ: She reads them for me. The razed towns, the
smashed machines, the looted industry, the steep
rise in unemployment and tuberculosis, and the
sharp fall in the birth rate. Nothing escapes me. My
sister copies out all the statistics. (*Pointing to the
drawer of the table*) They are all filed in this drawer.
The finest murder in history. I have all the proofs.

If not in twenty years, then in fifty at the most the last German will be dead. Don't think I am complaining. We were defeated, and they are strangling us. It's impeccable. Perhaps you can understand that I have no desire to witness the butchery. I shall not make a tour of the destroyed cathedrals and the burned-out factories. I won't visit the families huddled in the cellars. I won't wander among the invalids, the slaves, the traitors, and the prostitutes. I imagine you are used to the sight, but I tell you frankly, I couldn't stand it. And the cowards, in my opinion, are those who can stand it. We should have won the war. By any means—I said by *any*, see?—or else disappear. Believe me, I would have had enough military courage to blow my brains out, but since the German people accept the agony imposed on them, I have decided that one voice shall remain to cry no. (*He suddenly becomes excited.*) No! *Not guilty!* (*Shouting*) No! (*Pause.*) That's it.

JOHANNA (*slowly, undecided*): The abject agony imposed on them . . .

FRANZ (*without taking his eyes off her*): I said, that's it, that's all.

JOHANNA (*bewildered*): Yes, that's it. That's all. (*Pause.*) Is that the only reason you shut yourself up?

FRANZ: The only reason. (*Pause. She is lost in thought.*) What's the matter? Finish your work. Have I frightened you?

JOHANNA: Yes.

FRANZ: Why, my dear?

JOHANNA: Because you are afraid.

FRANZ: Of you?

JOHANNA: Of what I am going to tell you. (*Pause.*) I would rather not know what I know.

FRANZ (*defiantly, mastering his anguish*): What do you know? (*She hesitates, and they look at each other searchingly.*) Well? What do you know? (*She does not reply. Pause. They look at each other and are afraid. There is a knock at the door: five, four, then twice three. FRANZ smiles vaguely. He stands up and goes to open one of the doors upstage. It reveals the bathroom. He speaks in a low voice*) It won't be for long.

JOHANNA (*speaking normally*): I won't hide.

FRANZ (*putting a finger to his lips*): Ssh! (*In a low voice*) If you stand on your dignity, you'll lose the benefit of your little scheme.

(*JOHANNA hesitates, then decides to enter the bathroom. The knock is repeated. FRANZ opens the door, and LENI enters carrying a tray.*)

LENI (*stunned*): Didn't you bolt the door?

FRANZ: No.

LENI: Why?

FRANZ (*curtly*): Are you questioning me? (*Quickly*) Give me that tray and stay there. (*He takes the tray from her and starts to carry it to the table.*)

LENI (*dumfounded*): What's come over you?

FRANZ: It's too heavy. (*He turns around and looks at her.*) Are you reproaching me for my good deeds?

LENI: No, but I am afraid of them. When you are good, I expect the worst.

FRANZ (*laughing*): Ha! Ha! (*LENI enters and closes the door behind her.*) I did not tell you to come in. (*Pause. He takes a wing of chicken and eats.*) Well, I am going to have my dinner. See you tomorrow.

LENI: Wait. I want to ask you to forgive me. It was I who picked the quarrel.

FRANZ (*his mouth full*): Quarrel?

LENI: Yes, when I was here before.

FRANZ (*vaguely*): Oh, yes! When you were here . . . (*Quickly*) Well, I forgive you. There!

LENI: I told you that I was afraid of despising you. I didn't mean it.

FRANZ: Perfect! Perfect! Everything is perfect. (*He eats.*)

LENI: I accept your Crabs. I submit to their judgment. Shall I tell them? (*To Crabs*) Crustaceans, I worship you.

FRANZ: What's come over you?

LENI: I don't know. (*Pause.*) There is something else I want to tell you. I need you—you, the heir to our name, the only one whose caresses stir me without humiliating me. (*Pause.*) I don't amount to anything, but I was born a Gerlach, which means I am mad with pride—and I cannot make love to anyone but a Gerlach. Incest is my law and my fate. (*Laughing*) It's my way of strengthening the family ties.

FRANZ (*imperiously*): Enough. Psychology tomorrow. (*She starts. She is defiant again and observes him closely.*) We are reconciled, I give you my word. (*Pause.*) Tell me, the hunchback . . .

LENI (*taken by surprise*): What hunchback?

FRANZ: Werner's wife. Is she pretty at least?

LENI: Ordinary.

FRANZ: I see. (*Pause. Seriously*) Thank you, little sister. You have done what you could. Everything you could. (*He leads her back to the door. She allows herself to be led, but remains anxious.*) I have not been a very easy patient, eh? Goodbye!

LENI (*trying to laugh*): How solemn you are! I'll see you tomorrow, you know.

FRANZ (*softly, almost tenderly*): I hope so with all my heart.

(*He opens the door. He bends and kisses her forehead. She raises her head and quickly kisses him on the mouth and goes out. He closes the door, bolts it, takes out his handkerchief, and wipes his lips. He goes back to the table.*)

FRANZ: Don't be taken in, comrades, Leni *cannot* lie. (*Pointing to the bathroom*) The liar is in there. I am going to tie her up in knots, eh? Don't worry, I know more than one trick. This evening you will see the downfall of a false witness. (*He notices that his hands are trembling and makes a violent effort to control himself as he continues to gaze at his hands.*) Come on, boys, come on! There! There! (*His hands gradually stop trembling. With a quick glance in the mirror, he straightens his uniform and adjusts his Sam Browne belt. He has changed. For the first time since the beginning of the scene, he is fully master of himself. He goes to the bathroom door, opens it, and bows.*) To work, madame!

(*JOHANNA enters. He closes the door and follows her, intently, on the alert. Throughout the following scene it is obvious that he is trying to dominate her. He goes and places himself in front of JOHANNA, who has taken a step toward the entrance. She stops.*)

FRANZ: Don't move. Leni hasn't left the drawing room.

JOHANNA: What is she doing there?

FRANZ: Tidying up. (*She takes another step.*) Your heels. (*He imitates the noise of a woman's heels with little blows against the door. As he speaks, his eyes never leave her face. One feels that he is measur-*

ing the risk he is running, and that his words are calculated.) You wanted to leave, but wasn't there something you wanted to tell me?

(JOHANNA *seems ill at ease since she has come out of the bathroom.*)

JOHANNA: No, there wasn't.

FRANZ: Oh? (*Pause.*) Haven't you anything to say?

JOHANNA: No, I haven't.

FRANZ (*gets up abruptly*): No, my dear sister-in-law, that would be too easy. She was going to set me free, and now she has changed her mind and is going away forever, leaving behind her carefully planted doubts to poison me. I'll have none of that! (*He goes to the table, takes two champagne glasses and a bottle. As he pours the champagne into the glasses*) Is it Germany? Has she recovered? Are we swimming on the tide of prosperity?

JOHANNA (*exasperated*): Germany . . .

FRANZ (*very quick, covering his ears*): Useless! Useless! I will not believe you. (JOHANNA *looks at him, shrugs her shoulders, and is silent. He walks about airily and quite at ease.*) In fact, it has failed.

JOHANNA: What has?

FRANZ: Your escapade.

JOHANNA: Yes. (*Pause. In a gloomy voice*) It was kill or cure.

FRANZ: Oh, yes! (*Amiably*) You will find something else. (*Pause.*) At any rate, you have given me the pleasure of looking at you, and I must thank you for your generosity.

JOHANNA: I am not generous.

FRANZ: What would you call all the trouble you have taken? All that work in front of the mirror? That must have taken you several hours. What a lot of preparation for one man!

JOHANNA: I do it every evening.

FRANZ: For Werner.

JOHANNA: For Werner, and sometimes for his friends.

FRANZ (*shakes his head and smiles*): No.

JOHANNA: Do I drag around like a slattern in my room? Do I neglect myself?

FRANZ: Not that either. (*He stops looking at her and turns his eyes to the wall, describing what he imagines.*) You stand very straight. Very straight. To keep your head above water. Hair drawn back. Lips unpainted. Not a grain of powder. Werner has the right to be looked after, to tenderness, to kisses—to smiles, never. You do not smile any more.

JOHANNA (*smiling*): Visionary!

FRANZ: A recluse has special powers of vision which let him recognize his kind.

JOHANNA: They cannot meet very often.

FRANZ: Well, you see, it does happen sometimes.

JOHANNA: You recognize me?

FRANZ: We recognize each other.

JOHANNA: Am I a recluse? (*She gets up and looks at herself in the glass, then turns around, very beautiful, provocative for the first time.*) I would not have believed it. (*She goes to him.*)

FRANZ (*quickly*): Your heels!

(JOHANNA *takes off her shoes, smiling as she does so, and throws them, one after another, at the portrait of Hitler.*)

JOHANNA (*near* FRANZ): I saw the daughter of one of Werner's clients—chained up, weighing about eighty pounds, covered in lice. Do I look like her?

FRANZ: Like a sister. She wanted everything, I suppose. That's a losing game. She lost everything and locked herself up in her room so that it would look as if she refused everything.

JOHANNA (*irritated*): Are we going to talk about me for long? (*She steps back and points to the floor.*) Leni must have left the drawing room.

FRANZ: Not yet.

JOHANNA (*with a quick glance at her wrist watch*): Werner will be back. It's eight o'clock.

FRANZ (*violently*): No! (*She looks at him in surprise.*) Never mention the time here—eternity. (*He calms down.*) Patience, you will soon be free. (*Pause.*)

JOHANNA (*a mixture of defiance and curiosity*): So I lock myself up?

FRANZ: Yes.

JOHANNA: Through pride?

FRANZ: Certainly!

JOHANNA: What's missing?

FRANZ: You were not beautiful enough.

JOHANNA (*smiling*): Flatterer!

FRANZ: I am saying what you think.

JOHANNA: And you? What do you think?

FRANZ: Of myself?

JOHANNA: Of me.

FRANZ: That you are possessed.

JOHANNA: Mad?

FRANZ: Raving.

JOHANNA: What are you telling me? Your life story or mine?

FRANZ: Ours.

JOHANNA: What possessed you?

FRANZ: Has it a name? Emptiness. (*Pause.*) Let's say

—grandeur. . . . (*He laughs.*) It possessed me, but I didn't possess it.

JOHANNA: So that's it!

FRANZ: You watched yourself, eh? You tried to surprise yourself? (JOHANNA *nods.*) Did you catch yourself?

JOHANNA: What do you think? (*She glances at the mirror uneasily.*) I saw that. (*She points to her reflection. Pause.*) I used to go to the movies in the neighborhood. When the star Johanna Thies slid onto the far wall, I used to hear a little murmur. They were moved, each one by the other's emotion. I would look. . . .

FRANZ: And then?

JOHANNA: Then nothing. I never saw what they saw. (*Pause.*) What about you?

FRANZ: I was the same as you. I was a failure. I was decorated in front of the whole army. Does Werner find you beautiful?

JOHANNA: I certainly hope not. Just think! One man. Does that count?

FRANZ (*slowly*): I find you beautiful.

JOHANNA: Well, I hope you enjoy it, but don't talk about it. No one, you understand, no one, since the public rejected me . . . (*She calms down a little and laughs.*) You take yourself for a whole army corps.

FRANZ: Why not? (*He does not take his eyes from her.*) You must believe me. It's your chance. If you believe me, I become invulnerable.

JOHANNA (*laughing nervously*): It's a bargain. "Share my madness, and I will share yours."

FRANZ: Why not? You have nothing more to lose. As for my madness, you have been sharing that for a long time. (*Pointing to the door of the room*) When I opened the door to you, it wasn't me that you saw; it was a reflection in the depths of my eyes.

JOHANNA: Because they are empty.

FRANZ: For that very reason.

JOHANNA: I no longer remember what the photograph of a faded star was like. Everything disappeared when you spoke.

FRANZ: You spoke first.

JOHANNA: I couldn't stand it. I had to break the silence.

FRANZ: To break the spell.

JOHANNA: In any case, it turned out all right. (*Pause.*) What's the matter with you? (*She laughs nervously.*) It's like the lens of a camera. Stop! You're dead.

FRANZ: At your service. Death mirrors death. My grandeur reflects your beauty.

JOHANNA: I wanted to please the living.

FRANZ: The downtrodden mob that dreams of dying? You showed them the pure and tranquil face of eternal rest. The cinemas are cemeteries, my dear. What is your name?

JOHANNA: Johanna.

FRANZ: Johanna, I do not desire you, I do not love you. I am your witness and that of all mankind. I bear witness before the centuries, and I say: you are beautiful.

JOHANNA (*as though spellbound*): Yes.

(*He strikes the table violently.*)

FRANZ (*in a hard voice*): Confess that you have lied. Say that Germany is on its deathbed.

JOHANNA (*starts almost painfully*): Ha! (*She shudders, her face tense. She suddenly becomes almost ugly.*) You have spoiled everything.

FRANZ: Everything. I have shattered the image. (*Ab-*

ruptly) And you would like to bring me back to life? You would smash the mirror for nothing. I would go down among you. I would have my meals with the family, and you would go to Hamburg with your Werner. Where will that lead us?

JOHANNA (*She has gained control of herself. Smiling*): To Hamburg.

FRANZ: You will never be beautiful there again.

JOHANNA: No. Never again.

FRANZ: Here you will be beautiful every day.

JOHANNA: Yes, if I come to see you every day.

FRANZ: You will come.

JOHANNA: Will you open the door?

FRANZ: I shall open it.

JOHANNA (*imitating him*): Where will that lead us?

FRANZ: Here, into eternity.

JOHANNA (*smiling*): A double delirium . . . (*She is thinking. The spell has gone. One feels that she has returned to her original plans.*) Good. I shall come back.

FRANZ: Tomorrow?

JOHANNA: Perhaps tomorrow.
(*Pause.*)

FRANZ (*softly*): Say that Germany is on its deathbed. Say it, or else the mirror is in pieces. (*He gets excited, his hands begin to tremble again.*) Say it! Say it! Say it!

JOHANNA (*slowly*): A double delirium—very well. (*Pause.*) Germany is on its deathbed.

FRANZ: Is it really true?

JOHANNA: Yes.

FRANZ: They are strangling us?

JOHANNA: Yes.

FRANZ: Right. (*He cocks his ear.*) She has gone. (*He*

goes to pick up JOHANNA'S *shoes, kneels down in front of her, and puts them on her feet. She stands up. He gets up and bows, clicking his heels.*) See you tomorrow! (JOHANNA *goes as far as the door. He follows her, draws the bolt, and opens the door. She nods to him with the hint of a smile on her lips. She is about to leave when he stops her.*) Wait! (*She turns around, and he looks at her with sudden defiance.*) Who has won?

JOHANNA: Won what?

FRANZ: The first round.

JOHANNA: Guess.

(*She goes out. He closes the door, bolts and bars it. He seems relieved. He goes back to the middle of the room and stops.*)

FRANZ: Ah! (*The smile remains a moment, then his features become tense. He is afraid.*) De profundis clamavi! (*He is overwhelmed by suffering.*) Grind! Grind! Grind away! (*He begins to tremble.*)

CURTAIN

ACT III

WERNER's *office. Modern furniture. A mirror. Two doors.
The stage is empty. There is a knock at the door. Another knock, then the* FATHER *enters. He is carrying a
briefcase in his left hand, and his raincoat is folded
over his right arm. He closes the door, places his raincoat and briefcase on an armchair, then, as an after-
thought, goes back to the door and reopens it.*

FATHER (*calling offstage*): I can see you. (*A short
silence.*) Leni!
(LENI *appears after a moment.*)
LENI (*with a touch of defiance*): Here I am!
FATHER (*stroking her hair*): Hello. You were hiding?
LENI (*drawing back slightly*): Hello, father. Yes, I was
hiding. (*She looks at him.*) Look at you!
FATHER: The journey has made me flushed. (*He coughs
—a short dry cough that hurts.*)
LENI: Is there flu in Leipzig?
FATHER (*not understanding*): Flu? (*He understands.*)
No. I'm coughing. (*She looks at him in a kind of
fear.*) What's that got to do with you?
LENI (*turning and looking into space*): Nothing at all,
I hope. (*Pause.*)
FATHER (*jovially*): So, you were spying on me?
LENI (*amiably*): Yes, I was spying on you. It's my turn.
FATHER: You don't lose any time. I've only just arrived.
LENI: I wanted to know what you'd do when you
arrived.

FATHER: You can see, I'm visiting Werner.

LENI (*glancing at her wrist watch*): You know very well that Werner is down at the yard.

FATHER: I'll wait for him.

LENI (*pretending amazement*): You?

FATHER: Why not? (*He sits down.*)

LENI: Of course, why not? (*She sits down also.*) Shall I wait with you?

FATHER: I'll wait alone.

LENI: All right. (*She stands up.*) What have you been up to?

FATHER (*astonished*): In Leipzig?

LENI: Here.

FATHER (*astonished again*): What have I been up to?

LENI: That's what I'm asking you.

FATHER: I've been away for six days, my child.

LENI: What did you do on Sunday evening?

FATHER: You get on my nerves. (*Pause.*) Nothing. I had dinner and I went to bed.

LENI: Everything has changed. Why?

FATHER: What has changed?

LENI: You know.

FATHER: I've just come from the plane. I know nothing, and I've seen nothing.

LENI: You can see me.

FATHER: Exactly. (*Pause.*) You'll never change, Leni, no matter what happens.

LENI (*pointing to the mirror*): Father! I can see myself too. (*She goes over to the mirror.*) Of course, you've ruined my hair. (*She smooths her hair.*) When I see myself . . .

FATHER: You don't recognize yourself any more?

LENI: Not any more. (*She lets her arms fall, surprised*

as she looks at herself without illusions.) How futile!
(*Without turning from the mirror*) At dinner last
night Johanna was wearing make-up.

FATHER: Ah? (*His eyes glitter for a moment, then he
recovers.*) Well?

LENI: That's all.

FATHER: All women use make-up these days.

LENI: But she never does.

FATHER: She probably wants to win her husband back.

LENI: Her husband! (*With a sneer*) You didn't see
her eyes.

FATHER (*smiling*): What about them?

LENI (*pointedly*): You'll see. (*Pause. With a short
laugh*) Ah, you won't recognize anyone. Werner
talks in a loud voice, and he eats and drinks enough
for four men.

FATHER: It's not I who have changed you all.

LENI: Who else?

FATHER: No one. The vagaries of this old windpipe of
mine. Well, when a father departs . . . But what
are you complaining about? I've given you six
months' warning. You'll have time to make the best
of it, and you ought to thank me.

LENI: Thank you. (*Pause. In a changed voice*) On
Sunday evening you planted a time bomb in our
midst. Where is it? (*The* FATHER *shrugs his shoulders
and smiles.*) I'll find it.

FATHER: A bomb! Why should you . . . ?

LENI: The great ones of this world can't bear to die
alone.

FATHER: Am I going to blow up the whole family?

LENI: The family, no. You don't love it enough for
that. (*Pause.*) Franz.

FATHER: Poor Franz! Would I carry just him with me to my grave when the whole universe will survive me? Leni, I hope that you will stop me.

LENI: You can count on me. (*She takes a step toward him.*) If anyone attempts to go near him, you'll depart right away, and alone.

FATHER: Good. (*Pause. He sits down.*) Have you nothing more to tell me? (*She shakes her head. He speaks with authority, but without changing his tone.*) Go! (LENI *looks at him for a moment, bows her head, and goes out. The* FATHER *gets up, goes to the door and opens it, glances into the corridor as though to make sure that* LENI *is not hiding there, closes the door, turns the key in the lock, and places his handkerchief over the key in order to cover the keyhole. He crosses the room, goes to the door at the other end, opens it, and calls in a loud voice.*) Johanna!

(*He is interrupted by a fit of coughing. He turns around. Now that he is alone, he no longer keeps a firm hand on himself, and he is visibly suffering. He goes to the desk, takes a carafe, pours himself a glass of water, and drinks it.* JOHANNA *enters by the upstage door behind him.*)

JOHANNA: What is it? (*He turns around.*) Oh, it's you!

FATHER (*in a choking voice*): Yes, it is. (*He kisses her hand. His voice becomes firmer.*) Weren't you expecting me?

JOHANNA: I had forgotten about you. (*She recovers herself and laughs.*) Have you had a good trip?

FATHER: Excellent. (*She looks at the handkerchief covering the key.*) That's nothing. Just to blind someone. (*Pause. He looks at her.*) You're not wearing make-up.

JOHANNA: No.

FATHER: Aren't you going to see Franz?

JOHANNA: I'm not going to see anyone. I'm waiting for my husband.

FATHER: But you have seen him?

JOHANNA: Who?

FATHER: My son.

JOHANNA: You have two sons, and I don't know which one you are talking about.

FATHER: The elder. (*Pause.*) Well, my child?

JOHANNA (*with a start*): Father?

FATHER: What of our agreement?

JOHANNA (*with an air of amused surprise*): That's true; you have your rights. What a farce. (*Almost in confidence*) Everything is a farce on the ground floor, even you who are going to die. How do you manage to keep that rational expression? (*Pause.*) I'm sure you will understand nothing.

(*He was expecting this, but is unable to avoid a certain anguish in hearing it.*)

FATHER: You saw Franz? (*Pause.*) When? Monday?

JOHANNA: Monday, and every day since.

FATHER: Every day! (*Astounded*) Five times?

JOHANNA: I suppose so. I haven't counted.

FATHER: Five times. (*Pause.*) It's a miracle. (*He rubs his hands.*)

JOHANNA (*authoritatively, but without raising her voice*): Please! (*The* FATHER *puts his hands in his pockets.*) Don't look so pleased.

FATHER: You must excuse me, Johanna. Coming back on the plane, I was in a cold sweat. I thought everything was lost.

JOHANNA: Well?

FATHER: And now I hear that you see him every day.

JOHANNA: It is I who have lost everything.

FATHER: Why? (*She shrugs her shoulders.*) My child, since he opens his door to you, you must get on well with each other.

JOHANNA: We get on well. (*In a hard and cynical voice*) We're as thick as thieves.

FATHER (*disconcerted*): What? (*Pause.*) At least you're good friends?

JOHANNA: Anything but friends.

FATHER: Anything? (*Pause.*) You mean . . .

JOHANNA (*surprised*): What? (*She bursts into laughter.*) Lovers? Would you believe it, we haven't even thought of it. Was it necessary for your plans?

FATHER (*with some irritation*): Excuse me, daughter-in-law, but it's your fault. You explain nothing to me because you have made up your mind that I wouldn't understand.

JOHANNA: There's nothing to explain.

FATHER (*worried*): He isn't . . . ill, is he?

JOHANNA: Ill? (*She understands. With crushing contempt*) Oh, mad? (*Shrugging her shoulders*) How should I know?

FATHER: You see him in the flesh.

JOHANNA: If he's mad, so am I. And why shouldn't I be?

FATHER: In any case, you can tell me if he is unhappy.

JOHANNA (*amused*): Oh, that! (*In confidence*) Words don't have the same meaning up there.

FATHER: I see. How do you say that you're suffering up there?

JOHANNA: Nobody is suffering.

FATHER: Oh?

JOHANNA: One is kept busy.

FATHER: Franz is kept busy? (JOHANNA *nods.*) At what?

JOHANNA: At what? You mean by whom?

FATHER: Yes, that's what I mean. Well?

JOHANNA: That's none of my business.

FATHER (*gently*): Don't you want to talk to me about him?

JOHANNA (*with a profound weariness*): In what language? I have to translate all the time, and that makes me tired. (*Pause.*) I'm going away, father.

FATHER: Will you abandon him?

JOHANNA: He doesn't need anyone.

FATHER: Naturally, you have the right; you are free. (*Pause.*) You made me a promise.

JOHANNA: I've kept it.

FATHER: He knows. . . . (JOHANNA *nods.*) What did he say?

JOHANNA: That you smoked too much.

FATHER: What else?

JOHANNA: Nothing else.

FATHER (*deeply hurt*): I knew it! She lies to him all along the line, the bitch. What she must have told him during these thirteen years. . . .

(JOHANNA *laughs softly. He stops short and looks at her.*)

JOHANNA: Now you see that you don't understand! (*He looks at her sternly.*) What do you think I do with Franz? I lie to him.

FATHER: You?

JOHANNA: I lie to him every time I open my mouth.

FATHER (*amazed and almost disarmed*): But . . . you always hated lying.

JOHANNA: I still do.

FATHER: Well?

JOHANNA: Well, so I lie. To Werner in silence, to Franz in words.

FATHER (*curtly*): That's not what we agreed upon.

JOHANNA: No, it isn't.

FATHER: You were right; I . . . I don't understand. You're working against your own interests.

JOHANNA: Against Werner's.

FATHER: Which are yours.

JOHANNA: I no longer know.

(*Silence. The* FATHER, *bewildered for a moment, recovers.*)

FATHER: Have you gone over to the other side?

JOHANNA: There are no sides.

FATHER: Good. Then listen to me. Franz is greatly to be pitied, and I can understand that you wanted to spare him. But you can't go on like that. If you allow yourself to be affected by the pity you feel for him . . .

JOHANNA: We have no pity.

FATHER: We?

JOHANNA: Yes, Leni and I.

FATHER: Leni is another matter. But you, daughter-in-law, whatever you choose to call your feelings, don't lie to my son any more. You degrade him. (*She smiles. He speaks more sharply.*) He has only one desire: to run away. If you smother him with your lies, he'll let himself go under.

JOHANNA: I haven't time to do him much harm. I've told you, I'm going away.

FATHER: When and where?

JOHANNA: Tomorrow. Anywhere.

FATHER: With Werner?

JOHANNA: I don't know.

FATHER: Running away?

JOHANNA: Yes.

FATHER: But why?

JOHANNA: Two languages, two lives, two truths—don't you think that's too much for one person? (*She laughs.*) The orphans of Düsseldorf—well, I shall never get rid of them.

FATHER: What's that? A lie?

JOHANNA: A truth up there. They are abandoned children; they are dying of hunger in a camp. They must exist somehow or other, since they pursue me down to the ground floor. Yesterday evening I almost asked Werner if we couldn't save them. (*She laughs.*) That wouldn't mean anything. But up there . . .

FATHER: Well?

JOHANNA: I'm my own worst enemy. My voice lies, and my body contradicts it. I talk about the famine, and I say that we are dying of starvation. Look at me now! Do I look starved? If Franz saw me . . .

FATHER: Doesn't he see you, then?

JOHANNA: He hasn't got around to looking at me yet. (*As though speaking to herself*) A traitor. Inspired. Convincing. He speaks, and you listen. Then, suddenly, he sees himself in the glass; a placard across his chest with a single word on it that can be read even when he says nothing—treachery. That's the nightmare waiting for me daily in your son's room.

FATHER: It's everybody's nightmare. Every day and every night. (*Pause.*)

JOHANNA: Can I ask you a question? (*The FATHER nods.*) What has all this to do with me? Why have you dragged me into it?

FATHER (*sharply*): You're out of your mind, daughter-in-law. It was you who decided to become involved.

JOHANNA: How did you know I decided to?

FATHER: I didn't know.

JOHANNA: Don't lie, you who reproached me for lying. At any rate, don't lie too soon. Six days is a long time. You have given me time to think. (*Pause.*) The family conference was held especially for me.

FATHER: No, my child—for Werner.

JOHANNA: Werner? Bah! You attacked him so that I would defend him. It was I who had the idea of talking to Franz, I agree. Or, rather, it was I who found the idea. You had hidden it in the room, and you guided me so skillfully that I eventually found it staring me in the face. Isn't that true?

FATHER: I *did* wish that you would meet my son—for reasons that you well know.

JOHANNA (*vehemently*): For reasons that I don't know. (*Pause.*) When you brought us together—I who know and he who doesn't know—did you warn me that one word would be enough to kill him?

FATHER (*with dignity*): Johanna, I know nothing about my son.

JOHANNA: Nothing, except that he is trying to run away and that we are helping him do it with our lies. Come, now, you want to have it both ways. I tell you that one word is enough to kill him, and you don't even flinch.

FATHER (*smiling*): What word, my child?

JOHANNA (*laughing in his face*): Wealth.

FATHER: I beg your pardon?

JOHANNA: That or any other word which conveys the meaning that we are the richest nation in Europe. (*Pause.*) You don't seem very surprised.

FATHER: I'm not. Twelve years ago I became aware of my son's fears through certain remarks that he let fall. He believed that they wanted to wipe out Germany, and he shut himself up in order not to witness

our extermination. If it had been possible then to
reveal the future to him, he would have been cured
at once. Today it will be more difficult to save him.
He has acquired certain habits. Leni spoils him, and
a cloistered life has certain advantages. But never
fear, the only cure for his illness is the truth. He'll
take it badly at first, for it will remove all his pretexts
for sulking, but within a week he will be the first to
thank you.

JOHANNA (*vehemently*): What rubbish! (*Brutally*) I
saw him yesterday. Isn't that enough for you?

FATHER: No.

JOHANNA: Up there Germany is more dead than the
moon. If I bring it back to life, he will blow his
brains out.

FATHER (*laughing*): You don't say!

JOHANNA: I tell you that everything points that way.

FATHER: Does he no longer love his country?

JOHANNA: He worships it.

FATHER: Well, then, Johanna, that doesn't make good
sense.

JOHANNA: Oh, no, it doesn't. (*Laughing a little wildly*)
Good sense! (*Pointing to the* FATHER) That's what
you have in your head. I have his eyes in my head.
(*Pause.*) Stop everything! Your infernal machine is
going to blow up in your hands.

FATHER: I can't stop anything.

JOHANNA: Then I shall go away without seeing him
again, and for good. As for the truth, I shall tell it,
don't worry, but not to Franz. To Werner.

FATHER (*quickly*): No. (*Recovering himself*) You will
only hurt him.

JOHANNA: What else have I been doing since Sunday?
(*The sound of a car horn is heard in the distance.*)

There he is. He will know everything within a quarter of an hour.

FATHER (*commandingly*): Wait! (*She stops, taken aback. He goes to the door, removes the handkerchief and turns the key, then turns to face* JOHANNA.) I'll make you a proposition. (*She remains silent and tense. Pause.*) Say nothing to your husband. Go to see Franz one last time and tell him that I request an interview. If he accepts, I'll release Werner from his oath, and you shall *both* go whenever you wish. (*Pause.*) Johanna, I'm offering you freedom.

JOHANNA: I know.

(*The car enters the park.*)

FATHER: Well?

JOHANNA: I don't want it at that price.

FATHER: What price?

JOHANNA: Franz's death.

FATHER: My child, what has happened to you? It's like listening to Leni.

JOHANNA: It is. We are twin sisters. Don't be surprised; it's you who have made us the same. And if all the women in the world paraded in your son's room, they would be so many Lenis all lined up against you.

(*A sound of car brakes. The car stops in front of the steps.*)

FATHER: I beg you, don't decide yet! I promise you . . .

JOHANNA: It's no use. For hired killers, apply to the other sex.

FATHER: Will you tell Werner everything?

JOHANNA: Yes.

FATHER: Very well. And suppose I tell Leni everything?

JOHANNA (*amazed and frightened*): Tell Leni? You?

FATHER: Why not? The house would blow up.

JOHANNA (*on the edge of hysteria*): Blow the house up!
Blow the planet up! Then we should get some
peace at last. (*She starts to laugh, a low mirthless
laugh that increases in volume in spite of herself.*)
Peace! Peace! Peace!
(*There is a sound of footsteps in the corridor. The
FATHER goes rapidly to JOHANNA, seizes her roughly
by the shoulders, and shakes her, looking hard at her.
JOHANNA succeeds in calming herself. The FATHER
releases her and steps away from her just as the door
opens. WERNER enters quickly and sees his FATHER.*)

WERNER: Well!

FATHER: Hello, Werner.

WERNER: Hello, father. Pleased with your trip?

FATHER: Huh! (*He rubs his hands without being aware
that he is doing so.*) Pleased, yes, pleased. Perhaps
very pleased.

WERNER: You wanted to talk to me?

FATHER: To you? Oh, no. I'll leave you, children. (*At
the door*) Johanna, my proposition still stands. (*He
goes out.*)

WERNER: What proposition?

JOHANNA: I'll tell you.

WERNER: I don't like him to come nosing about in here.
(*He takes a bottle of champagne and two glasses
from a cupboard, places the glasses on the desk, and
begins to uncork the bottle.*) Champagne?

JOHANNA: No.

WERNER: Very well, I'll drink by myself. (*JOHANNA
takes the glasses away.*)

JOHANNA: Not this evening. I need you.

WERNER: You surprise me. (*He looks at her. Sharply*)
In any case, that doesn't prevent my drinking. (*He
releases the cork. JOHANNA utters a short cry. WERNER*

laughs, fills both glasses, and looks at her.) My word,
you're afraid!

JOHANNA: I'm a bit on edge.

WERNER (*with a kind of satisfaction*): I say that you're
afraid. (*Pause.*) Of whom? Father?

JOHANNA: Of him as well.

WERNER: And you want me to protect you? (*Laughing
derisively, but a little more relaxed*) The roles are
reversed. (*He drains his glass.*) Tell me what's
worrying you. (*Pause.*) Is it so difficult? Come on!
(*She does not move, but remains tense. He pulls her
toward him.*) Put your head on my shoulder. (*He
almost forces* JOHANNA's *head onto his shoulder.
Pause. He looks at himself in the mirror and smiles.*)
Back to normal. (*A short silence.*) Speak, my dear!

JOHANNA (*raising her head to look at him*): I've seen
Franz.

WERNER (*pushing her away angrily*): Franz! (*He turns
away from her, goes to the desk, pours himself another glass of champagne, calmly drinks, then turns
back to her, cool and smiling.*) That's good! Now you
know the whole family. (*She looks at him uneasily.*)
How do you find my elder brother? Quite a dandy,
eh? (*She looks at him, bewildered, and shakes her
head.*) Well! (*Amused*) Well, well. Is he in a bad
way? (*She has difficulty in speaking.*) Eh?

JOHANNA: You're taller than he.

WERNER (*still amused*): Ha! Ha! (*Pause.*) And does he
still wear his fine officer's uniform?

JOHANNA: It's no longer a fine uniform.

WERNER: Rags? But, tell me, poor old Franz is in pretty
bad shape, then? (JOHANNA *maintains a tense silence.
He picks up the glass.*) To his cure. (*He raises his
glass, then, seeing that she has no glass, goes to get

the other one and holds it out to her.) Let's drink a toast. (*She hesitates. Commandingly*) Take this glass. (*Her expression hardens as she takes it.*)

JOHANNA (*defiantly*): I drink to Franz!

(*She tries to clink her glass against* WERNER's, *but he quickly draws his glass away. They look at each other for a moment, nonplused, then* WERNER *bursts out laughing and throws the contents of his glass on the floor.*)

WERNER (*with violent abandon*): It's not true! It's not true! (JOHANNA *is amazed. He goes toward her.*) You've never seen him. You didn't take me in for a moment. (*Laughing in her face.*) What about the bolt, dear? And the iron bar? They have a signal; you can be sure of that.

JOHANNA (*who has regained her icy calm*): They have. I know it.

WERNER (*still laughing*): You do! I suppose you asked Leni.

JOHANNA: I asked your father.

WERNER (*astonished*): Ah! (*A long silence. He goes to the desk, puts down his glass, and thinks. Then he turns back to* JOHANNA. *He has maintained his jovial manner, but it is clear that he is making a great effort to control himself.*) Well, it was bound to happen. (*Pause.*) Father never does anything without reason. What is his interest in this affair?

JOHANNA: I'd like to know.

WERNER: What was it he proposed to you just now?

JOHANNA: He'll release you from your oath if Franz will grant him an interview.

(WERNER *has become gloomy and suspicious, and his suspicion increases during the ensuing dialogue.*)

WERNER: An interview. . . . And will Franz grant it?

JOHANNA (*with assurance*): Yes.

WERNER: And then?

JOHANNA: Nothing. We shall be free.

WERNER: Free to do what?

JOHANNA: To go away.

WERNER (*with a harsh laugh*): To Hamburg?

JOHANNA: Wherever we please.

WERNER: Perfect! (*With a harsh laugh*) Well, my wife, that's the best kick in the pants I've ever had.

JOHANNA (*amazed*): Werner, your father isn't thinking for a moment—

WERNER: Of his younger son? You bet he isn't. Franz will take my desk, he will sit in my armchair and drink my champagne, he will throw his oyster shells under my bed. Apart from that, who will think of me? Do I matter? (*Pause.*) The old man has changed his mind, that's all.

JOHANNA: But don't you understand anything?

WERNER: I understand that he wants to put my brother in charge of the firm. And I understand that you have deliberately acted as an intermediary for them. So long as you can clear out of here, you don't care if I'm kicked out. (JOHANNA *looks at him coldly. She lets him go on without attempting to make her own point.*) They break up my lawyer's practice to put me under house arrest in this frightful building, surrounded by the dear memories of my childhood. Then, one fine day, the prodigal son consents to leave his room. They kill the fatted calf, kick me out of doors, and everybody is satisfied, starting with my wife! A wonderful story, isn't it? You can tell it all over Hamburg. (*He goes to the desk, pours himself a glass of champagne, and drinks it. He becomes increasingly drunk up to the end of the Act.*) All the

same, it would be well for you not to pack your bags
yet, because, you see, I'm not sure that I'll let them
get away with it. (*Loudly*) I have the firm, and I'm
keeping it. They'll see what I'm made of. (*He sits
down at the desk and speaks in a calm and malicious
voice with a hint of self-importance.*) Now leave me
alone. I have to think. (*Pause.*)

JOHANNA (*slowly and in a cold and calm voice*): It's
not a question of the firm. No one wants to take that
from you.

WERNER: No one except my father and his son.

JOHANNA: Franz won't take charge of the firm.

WERNER: Why not?

JOHANNA: He doesn't want to.

WERNER: He doesn't *want* to, or is it because he *can't*?

JOHANNA (*against her will*): Both. (*Pause.*) And your
father knows it.

WERNER: Then, why?

JOHANNA: Because he wants to see Franz again before
he dies.

WERNER (*slightly relieved but defiant*): It sounds
crooked.

JOHANNA: Very crooked, but it's no concern of yours.
(WERNER *stands up and goes to her. He looks straight
into her eyes, and she returns his look.*)

WERNER: I believe you. (*He drinks.* JOHANNA, *annoyed,
turns her head away.*) Good for nothing. (*He
laughs.*) And a weakling into the bargain. On Sunday
father spoke about unhealthy fat.

JOHANNA (*quickly*): Franz is nothing but skin and
bone.

WERNER: Yes, with a shrunken stomach, like all prisoners. (*He looks at himself in the mirror and, almost
unconsciously, throws out his chest.*) Good-for-noth-

ing. In rags. Half-cracked. (*He turns toward* JO-
HANNA.) Have you seen him . . . often?

JOHANNA: Every day.

WERNER: I wonder what you find to say to each other.
(*He moves with new assurance.*) "There's no tree
without a rotten branch." I can't remember who said
that. Terrible, but true, eh? Only up to now I thought
I was the rotten branch. (*Placing his hands on*
JOHANNA's *shoulders*) Thank you, my dear wife,
you have rescued me. (*He goes to take his glass, but
she prevents him.*) You're right—no more champagne. (*He sweeps the two glasses off with his hand,
and they break on the floor.*) Send him some bottles
from me. (*He laughs.*) As for you, you won't see him
again. I forbid you.

JOHANNA (*still icy*): Very well. Take me away from
here.

WERNER: I tell you that you've rescued me. I was
imagining things, you know. From now on everything
will be all right.

JOHANNA: Not for me.

WERNER: No? (*He looks at her. His face changes and
his shoulders slump slightly.*) Even if I swear to you
that I'll turn over a new leaf and put them all in
their place?

JOHANNA: Not even then.

WERNER (*sharply*): You two have been making love!
(*A short laugh.*) Say it; I won't mind. He only had
to whistle and he had all the women running after
him. (*He looks at her angrily.*) I asked you a question.

JOHANNA (*very hard*): If you were to force me to reply,
I should never forgive you.

WERNER: Reply and don't forgive.

JOHANNA. No.

WERNER: You don't make love. Good! But you're dying to do so.

JOHANNA (*coldly, but with a touch of hatred*): You're contemptible.

WERNER (*smiling and malicious*): I'm a Gerlach. Answer.

JOHANNA: No.

WERNER: Then what are you afraid of?

JOHANNA (*still icy*): Before I knew you, death and madness fascinated me. It's beginning all over again up there, and I don't want it to. (*Pause.*) I believe in his crabs more than he does.

WERNER: Because you love him.

JOHANNA: Because they're true. Madmen often speak the truth, Werner.

WERNER: Really? Which truth?

JOHANNA: There's only one: the horror of living. (*Recovering her warmth*) I can't stand it! I can't stand it! I prefer to lie to myself. If you love me, save me. (*Pointing to the ceiling*) That lid is crushing me. Take me to some town where everyone is the same, where they all lie to themselves. With a wind, a wind that comes from afar. We shall find each other again, Werner, I swear it.

WERNER (*with a sudden and savage violence*): Find each other again? Ha! And how could I have lost you, Johanna? I have never had you. But enough of that! I didn't need your sympathy. You cheated me on the deal. I wanted a wife, and I've only possessed her corpse. I don't care if you do go mad; we shall stay here. (*He mimics her.*) "Defend me! Save me!" How? By clearing out? (*He controls himself and smiles coldly and maliciously.*) I was carried away just now. Forgive me. You will do your best to be a good wife; that's your part in life. But the pleasure will be all yours. (*Pause.*) How far would we have to go for you to forget my brother? How far would we have to run? Trains, ships, planes; what a business, and how dreary! You'll look at everything with those empty eyes—the tragic woman—and that won't be much of a change for you. As for me, have you considered what I shall be thinking all that time? That I gave up from the start, and that I ran away without raising a finger. A coward, eh? A coward. That's what you would like me to be, and then you could comfort me. Maternally. (*Violently*) We'll stay here! Until one of the three of us dies—you, my brother, or me.

JOHANNA: How you hate me!

WERNER: I shall love you when I have won you. And I'm going to fight, don't worry. (*He laughs.*) I shall win. You only like strength, you women. And I'm the one who has strength.

(*He takes her by the waist and kisses her brutally. She strikes him with her clenched fists, releases herself, and bursts into laughter.*)

JOHANNA (*still laughing*): Oh, Werner, do you think he bites?

WERNER: Who? Franz?

JOHANNA: The hardened old soldier you're trying to ape. (*Pause.*) If we stay, I shall visit your brother every day.

WERNER: I don't doubt it. And you'll spend every night in my bed. (*He laughs.*) It'll be easy to make the comparison.

JOHANNA (*sadly and slowly*): Poor Werner! (*She goes toward the door.*)

WERNER (*suddenly bewildered*): Where are you going?

JOHANNA (*with a malicious laugh*): To make the comparison.
(*She opens the door and goes out. He makes no
effort to stop her.*)

CURTAIN

ACT IV

FRANZ's *room. The same décor as in Act Two, but all the placards have disappeared, leaving only the portrait of Hitler. There are no longer any oyster shells on the floor. There is a desk lamp on the table.* FRANZ *is alone.*

FRANZ: Masked inhabitants of the ceilings, your attention, please! Masked inhabitants of the ceilings, your attention, please! (*Pause. He looks at the ceiling.*) Eh? (*Under his breath*) I can't feel them. (*Loudly*) Comrades! Comrades! Germany is speaking to you. Martyred Germany. (*Pause. He becomes despondent.*) This audience is stone cold. (*He gets up and starts to walk about.*) Strange and unfounded impression. This evening, history is going to stop. Contact! The explosion of the planet is on the agenda, and the scientists have their finger on the button. Goodbye! (*Pause.*) Still, it would have been nice to know what would have become of the human race if it had survived. (*Angrily and almost violently*) I prostitute myself to please them, and they don't even listen. (*Warmly*) Dear listeners, I beg you, if I no longer have your ear, if the false witnesses have led you astray . . . (*Sharply*) Wait! (*He searches in his pocket.*) I have the culprit. (*He brings out a wrist watch and holds it in disgust by the end of the leather strap.*) I was given this beast as a present, and I was

foolish enough to accept it. (*He looks at it.*) Fifteen
minutes! Fifteen minutes late! Unpardonable. I'll
smash this watch. (*He puts it on his wrist.*) Fifteen
minutes. Sixteen now. (*Bursts out*) How can I pre-
serve my ageless patience if they annoy me with
pinpricks? It will all come to a sticky end. (*Pause.*)
It's quite simple; I won't open the door. I'll keep her
waiting two solid hours on the landing. (*There is a
triple knock at the door. He hurries to open it, then
steps back to allow* JOHANNA *to enter. He points to
his wrist watch.*) Seventeen!

JOHANNA: What?

FRANZ (*imitating a speaking clock*): Four hours, seventeen minutes, thirty seconds. Have you brought my
brother's photograph? (*Pause.*) Well?

JOHANNA (*unwillingly*): Yes.

FRANZ: Show it to me.

JOHANNA (*still hesitant*): What are you going to do
with it?

FRANZ (*with an insolent laugh*): What does one usually
do with a photograph?

JOHANNA (*after some hesitation*): Here it is.

FRANZ (*looking at it*): Well, I wouldn't have recognized
him. He's quite an athlete. Congratulations! (*He
puts the photograph in his pocket.*) And how are our
orphans?

JOHANNA (*at a loss*): Which orphans?

FRANZ: Come now! In Düsseldorf.

JOHANNA: Oh. . . . (*Quickly*) They're dead.

FRANZ (*addressing the ceiling*): Crabs, there were
seven hundred of them. Seven hundred poor kids
without hearth or home . . . (*He checks himself.*)
I'm fed up with those orphans, my dear. Let them
be buried as soon as possible. Good riddance.

(*Pause.*) You see! That's what I've become because of you—a bad German.

JOHANNA: Because of me?

FRANZ: I ought to have known that she would upset everything. It took me five years to drive time out of this room, and you only needed a moment to bring it back. (*He shows her the watch.*) This wheedling beast that purrs on my wrist and that I stuff into my pocket when I hear Leni knock at the door is universal time, the time of the speaking clock, of the timetables and the observatories. What am I supposed to do with it? Am I universal? (*Looking at the watch*) I find this gift suspect.

JOHANNA: Then give it back to me!

FRANZ: Oh, no! I'm keeping it. Only, I wonder why you gave it to me.

JOHANNA: Because I'm still living, just as you used to live.

FRANZ: What is living? Waiting for you? I wasn't expecting anything more for a thousand years. That lamp never goes out. Leni comes when she likes. I used to sleep off and on, when sleep overcame me. In short, I never knew what time it was. (*Peevishly*) Now I have the bustle of days and nights. (*Glancing at the watch*) Four twenty-five; the shadows are lengthening, and daylight is fading. I hate the afternoons. When you leave, it will be night, with the light on here, and I shall be afraid. (*Suddenly*) When are they going to bury the poor little things?

JOHANNA: On Monday, I believe.

FRANZ: They must have a memorial chapel in the open air, in the ruins of the church. Seven hundred little coffins mourned by a crowd dressed in rags! (*He looks at her.*) You haven't put on any make-up?

JOHANNA: You can see I haven't.

FRANZ: An oversight?

JOHANNA: No. I didn't intend to come.

FRANZ (*violently*): What?

JOHANNA: It's Werner's day. (*Pause.*) Yes, Saturday.

FRANZ: Why does he need a day when he has you
every night? Saturday? . . . Ah, yes, the week end.
(*Pause.*) And Sunday as well, of course.

JOHANNA: Of course.

FRANZ: If I understand you rightly, it's Saturday. Ah,
madame, the watch doesn't say so. You must give
me a calendar. (*He laughs harshly, then speaks
sharply*) Two days without you? Impossible!

JOHANNA: Do you think that I should deprive my
husband of the only moments when we can be
together?

FRANZ: Why not? (*She laughs, and does not reply.*)
Has he got rights over you? I'm sorry, but so have I.

JOHANNA (*with some violence*): You? None. Not in
the least.

FRANZ: Did I seek you out? (*Shouting*) When will
you understand that this trivial waiting about is
keeping me away from my job? The Crabs can't
understand, and they're getting suspicious. The false
witnesses are winning. (*Insultingly*) Delilah!

JOHANNA (*breaks into a sarcastic laugh and goes to
him. She looks at him insolently.*): And is this Samson? (*Laughing more than ever*) Samson! Samson!
(*She stops laughing.*) I imagined him to be quite
different.

FRANZ (*in a formidable voice*): I *am* Samson. I'm
carrying the centuries on my back, and if I straighten
up they will crash. (*Pause. He resumes his natural
voice and speaks with bitter irony*) Besides, I'm con-

vinced that he was a poor fellow. (*He walks across the room*). To be so dependent! (*Pause. He sits down.*) You annoy me, madame. (*Pause.*)

JOHANNA: I won't annoy you any more.

FRANZ: What have you done?

JOHANNA: I've told Werner everything.

FRANZ: Good heavens! Why?

JOHANNA (*bitterly*): I wonder.

FRANZ: Did he take it well?

JOHANNA: He took it very badly.

FRANZ (*upset and nervous*): Is he leaving us? Is he taking you away?

JOHANNA: He's staying here.

FRANZ (*reassured*): That's all right. (*He rubs his hands.*) Quite all right.

JOHANNA (*with bitter irony*): You never take your eyes off me! But what do you see? (*She goes over to him, takes his head between her hands, and forces him to look at her.*) Look at me! Yes, like that. Now dare to tell me that everything is quite all right.

FRANZ (*looks at her and releases himself*): I can see, yes, I can see. You miss Hamburg. The easy life. Being admired and desired by men. (*Shrugging his shoulders*) That's important to you.

JOHANNA (*sadly and dully*): Samson was just a poor fellow.

FRANZ: Yes, yes, yes. A poor fellow. (*He starts to walk sideways.*)

JOHANNA: What are you doing?

FRANZ (*in a deep, harsh voice*): I'm walking crab fashion. (*Amazed at what he has just said*) What's that? (*Coming back to her and speaking naturally*) Why am I a poor fellow?

JOHANNA: Because you don't understand anything.
(*Pause.*) We shall go through Hell.

FRANZ: Who?

JOHANNA: Werner, you, and me. (*A short pause.*)
He's staying here out of jealousy.

FRANZ (*amazed*): What?

JOHANNA: Out of jealousy. Is that clear? (*Pause. She
shrugs her shoulders.*) You don't even know what it
is. (FRANZ *laughs.*) He'll send me to you every day—
even Sunday. He'll make a martyr of himself at the
yard in his huge ministerial office, and I'll pay for it
every evening.

FRANZ (*genuinely surprised*): Pardon me, my dear,
but *who* is he jealous of? (*She shrugs her shoulders.
He takes out the photograph and looks at it.*) Of me?
(*Pause.*) Have you told him . . . what has become
of me?

JOHANNA: Yes, I have.

FRANZ: And what does he say?

JOHANNA: Well, he's jealous.

FRANZ: He's being completely unreasonable. I'm ill.
Mad, perhaps. I'm in hiding. The war has broken
me, madame.

JOHANNA: It hasn't broken your pride.

FRANZ: Is that enough to make him jealous of me?

JOHANNA: Yes.

FRANZ: Tell him that my pride is shattered. Tell him
that I boast as a defense. Wait! I'll debase myself
completely. Tell Werner that I'm jealous.

JOHANNA: Of him?

FRANZ: Of his freedom, of his muscles, of his smile,
of his wife, of his clear conscience. (*Pause.*) Well?
What a sop for his pride.

JOHANNA: He won't believe me.

FRANZ: That's his bad luck. (*Pause.*) What about you?

JOHANNA: Me?

FRANZ: Do you believe me?

JOHANNA (*uncertain and annoyed*): No, I don't.

FRANZ: There have been some indiscretions, madame. I know every minute of your private life.

JOHANNA (*shrugging her shoulders*): Leni lies to you.

FRANZ: Leni never talks about you. (*Pointing to his watch*) It's the chatterbox. It tells everything. It starts to talk as soon as you leave me. Half past eight, family dinner. Ten o'clock, everyone retires; cozy chat with your husband. Eleven o'clock, evening toilet. Werner goes to bed; you take a bath. Midnight, you get into his bed.

JOHANNA (*with an insolent laugh*): Into his bed? (*Pause.*) No.

FRANZ: Twin beds?

JOHANNA: Yes.

FRANZ: In which one do you make love?

JOHANNA (*exasperated, insolently*): Sometimes in one, sometimes in the other.

FRANZ (*growls*): Huh! (*He looks at the photograph.*) The athlete must crush you. Do you like that?

JOHANNA: If I chose it, it's because I prefer athletes to weaklings.

(FRANZ *looks at the photograph with a growl, then replaces it in his pocket.*)

FRANZ: I haven't slept a wink for sixty hours.

JOHANNA: Why?

FRANZ: You won't make love while I'm asleep.

JOHANNA (*with a dry laugh*): Then don't sleep any more.

FRANZ: I don't intend to. When he takes you tonight, you'll know that I'm awake.

JOHANNA (*angrily*): I am sorry to deprive you of your disgusting solitary pleasures. Sleep tonight. Werner won't touch me.

FRANZ (*disconcerted*): Oh!

JOHANNA: Are you disappointed?

FRANZ: No.

JOHANNA: He won't touch me again while we remain here because of him. (*Pause.*) Do you know what he thinks? That you have seduced me. (*Insultingly*) You! (*Pause.*) You two are alike.

FRANZ (*looking at the photograph*): We are not.

JOHANNA: Yes, you are. Two Gerlachs, two brothers living in a dream world. And what am I? Nothing. An instrument of torture. Each of you looks for the other's caresses on me. (*She comes up to him.*) Look at this body. (*She takes his hand and places it on her shoulder.*) When I lived among men, they didn't need black masses in order to desire it. (*She repulses him and breaks away. Pause. Abruptly*) Your father wants to speak to you.

FRANZ (*coldly*): Oh!

JOHANNA: If you will meet him, he will release Werner from his oath.

FRANZ (*calmly and coldly*): And what then? Will you go away?

JOHANNA: That will depend entirely on Werner.

FRANZ (*still coldly*): Do you want me to meet him?

JOHANNA: Yes.

FRANZ (*in the same tone*): And must I give up seeing you?

JOHANNA: Of course.

FRANZ (*maintaining his cold manner*): What will happen to me?

JOHANNA: You will go back to eternity.

FRANZ: All right. (*Pause.*) Go and tell my father. . . .

JOHANNA (*quickly*): No.

FRANZ: What?

JOHANNA (*heatedly*): No, I'll tell him nothing.

FRANZ (*impassive, thinking he has won*): I must give him my reply.

JOHANNA (*still angry*): It's no good. I won't tell him.

FRANZ: Then why did you convey his request?

JOHANNA: I didn't intend to.

FRANZ: Didn't intend to?

JOHANNA (*gives a short laugh and looks at him in hatred*): Just imagine, I wanted to kill you.

FRANZ (*amiably*): Oh! For how long?

JOHANNA: For the past five minutes.

FRANZ: And have you got over it now?

JOHANNA (*smiling and calm*): I still feel like scratching your face. (*She draws the fingers of both hands down his face, and he makes no attempt to prevent her.*) Like this. (*She drops her hands and breaks away from him.*)

FRANZ (*still amiable*): Five minutes. You're lucky. My desire to kill you lasts all night.

(*A short pause. She sits on the bed and looks into space, talking to herself.*)

JOHANNA: I won't ever go away again.

FRANZ (*watching her closely*): Never again?

JOHANNA (*without looking at him*): Never again.

(*She utters a short wild laugh, opens her hands as though to let something fall, and looks at her feet. FRANZ watches her, and his manner changes. He*

*again becomes the madman, still and aloof as in Act
Two.)*

FRANZ: Stay with me, then. All the time.

JOHANNA: In this room?

FRANZ: Yes.

JOHANNA: And never leave it? (FRANZ *nods.*) Lock myself up?

FRANZ: Yes. (*He walks about while speaking, and*
JOHANNA *watches him. As he continues speaking,
she recovers and hardens. She understands that* FRANZ
is merely seeking to protect his delirium.) I have lived
for twelve years on a roof of ice above the summits.
I had cast into the night the teeming baubles.

JOHANNA (*already suspicious*): What baubles?

FRANZ: The world, dear madame. The world where you
live. (*Pause.*) That jumble of iniquity lives again.
Through you. When you leave me, it surrounds me
because you are in it. You crush me at the foot of
Saxonian "Switzerland"; I rave in a hunting lodge
twenty feet above sea level. Water is reborn in the
bath around your flesh. Now the Elbe flows and the
grass grows. A woman is a traitor, madame.

JOHANNA (*in a low and hard voice*): If I am betraying
anyone, it is not you.

FRANZ: Yes, me. Me as well, you double agent. For
twenty hours out of twenty-four, you see, you feel,
and you think beneath the soles of my feet with all
the others. You subject me to ordinary laws. (*Pause.*)
If I have you under lock and key—absolute peace.
The world will return to the abyss, and you will be
nothing but what you are. (*Pointing at her*) That!
The Crabs will trust me again, and I shall speak to
them.

JOHANNA (*sarcastically*): Will you speak to me sometimes?

FRANZ (*pointing to the ceiling*): We shall speak to them together. (JOHANNA *bursts out laughing, and he looks at her in bewilderment.*) You refuse?

JOHANNA: What is there to refuse? You're relating a nightmare, and I'm listening. That's all.

FRANZ: Won't you leave Werner?

JOHANNA: I've told you I won't.

FRANZ: Then leave me. Here is your husband's photograph. (*He gives it to her and she takes it.*) As for the watch, it will enter eternity at the fourth stroke precisely. (*He undoes the strap and looks at the watch.*) There it goes! (*He throws it on the floor.*) From now on it will always be four thirty. In remembrance of you, madame. Goodbye. (*He goes to the door, draws the bolt, and lifts the bar. A long pause. He bows and shows her the door. She goes slowly to the door, pushes the bolt back, and lowers the bar. Then she comes up to him, calm and unsmiling, with authority.*) Good! (*Pause.*) What are you going to do?

JOHANNA: What I have been doing since Monday. A shuttle service.

FRANZ: And suppose I don't open the door?

JOHANNA (*calmly*): You will.

(FRANZ *stoops down, picks up the watch and holds it to his ear. His face changes and his voice takes on a certain warmth. From this point a real understanding is established between them for a time.*)

FRANZ: We're in luck; it's going. (*He looks at the watch.*) Four thirty-one; a minute past eternity. Turn, hands, turn. We have to live. (*To* JOHANNA) How?

JOHANNA: I don't know.

FRANZ: We shall be three raving lunatics.

JOHANNA: Four.

FRANZ: Four?

JOHANNA: If you refuse to meet your father, he'll tell Leni.

FRANZ: He's quite capable of it.

JOHANNA: What would happen?

FRANZ: Leni doesn't like complications.

JOHANNA: Well?

FRANZ: She'll simplify matters.

JOHANNA (*picking up the revolver, which is on* FRANZ'S *table*): With this?

FRANZ: With that, or some other way.

JOHANNA: In such cases, women shoot the woman.

FRANZ: Leni is only half a woman.

JOHANNA: Are you worried about dying?

FRANZ: Frankly, yes. (*Pointing to the ceiling*) I haven't yet found the words that they understand. What about you?

JOHANNA: I wouldn't want Werner to be left alone.

FRANZ (*with a short laugh, summing up*): We can neither live nor die.

JOHANNA (*in the same tone*): We can neither see each other nor leave each other.

FRANZ: We're in a hell of a fix. (*He sits down.*)

JOHANNA: We are.

(*She sits on the bed. Silence.* FRANZ *turns his back on her and rubs two oyster shells together.*)

FRANZ: There must be a way out.

JOHANNA: There isn't.

FRANZ (*fiercely*): There must be one. (*He rubs the shells together with a wild and desperate violence.*) Mustn't there?

JOHANNA: Put those shells down. I can't stand it.

FRANZ: Be quiet! (*He throws the shells against the portrait of Hitler.*) Look what an effort I'm making. (*He half turns toward her and shows her how his hands are trembling.*) Do you know what makes me afraid?

JOHANNA: The way out? (*He nods assent, still tense.*) What is it?

FRANZ: Take it easy. (*He stands up and walks about agitatedly.*) Don't hurry me. All roads are closed; there isn't even the choice of a lesser evil. But there is one road that's never closed, since it leads nowhere. The worst one. Shall we take it?

JOHANNA (*cries out*): No!

FRANZ: You see. You *do* know the way out.

JOHANNA (*passionately*): We've been happy.

FRANZ: Happy in hell?

JOHANNA (*taking him up, passionately*): Happy in hell, yes. In spite of ourselves. I beg you, I implore you, let us stay as we are. Let us wait without a word or a sign. (*She takes him by the arm.*) Don't let's change.

FRANZ: The others change, Johanna; the others will change us. (*Pause.*) Do you think Leni will let us live?

JOHANNA (*violently*): Leni! I'll take care of her. If there's any shooting to be done, I'll shoot first.

FRANZ: Let's forget about Leni. Here we are, alone and face to face. What will happen?

JOHANNA (*with the same passion*): Nothing will happen! Nothing will change! We shall be . . .

FRANZ: What will happen is that you will destroy me.

JOHANNA (*still passionately*): Never!

FRANZ: You will destroy me slowly, surely, by your

very presence. Already my madness is falling in ruins. It was my refuge, Johanna. What will become of me when I see the light of day?

JOHANNA (*passionately*): You will be cured.

FRANZ (*bursts out*): Ha! (*Pause. Harsh laugh.*) I shall be in my dotage.

JOHANNA: I shall never hurt you. I'm not thinking of curing you. Your madness is my cage. I turn around and around there.

FRANZ (*with a sad and bitter tenderness*): You turn around, little squirrel? Squirrels have good teeth. You will bite through the bars.

JOHANNA: It's not true! I don't even want to. I bow to all your whims.

FRANZ: Yes, you do, that's pretty obvious. But your lies give you away.

JOHANNA (*tense*): I never lie to you.

FRANZ: You do nothing but. Generously, virtuously, like a good little soldier. Only you lie very badly. To lie well, you have to be a lie yourself. That's what I am. You, you're true. When I look at you, I know that truth exists and that it's not on my side. (*Laughing*) If there are any orphans in Düsseldorf, I'll bet they're as fat as pigeons.

JOHANNA (*in a set and mechanical voice*): They are dead. Germany is dead.

FRANZ (*brutally*): Be quiet! (*Pause.*) Well? Do you know the worst road now? You open my eyes by trying to close them, and I become your accomplice every time I find you out, because . . . because I rely on you.

JOHANNA (*recovering a little*): So we do the opposite of what we want to do.

FRANZ: Exactly.

JOHANNA (*abruptly and scornfully*): Well? What's the way out?

FRANZ: Let us each want what we have to do.

JOHANNA: Then I must want to destroy you?

FRANZ: We must help each other to want the truth.

JOHANNA: You will never want that. You're a fake, right to the marrow of your bones.

FRANZ (*dry and distant*): I had to defend myself, my dear. (*Pause. More warmly*) I shall renounce my illusions when . . . (*He hesitates.*)

JOHANNA: When?

FRANZ: When I love you more than my lies, and when you love me in spite of my truth.

JOHANNA (*ironically*): Have you a truth? What is it? What you tell the Crabs?

FRANZ (*pouncing on her words*): What crabs? Are you mad? What crabs? (*Pause. He turns away.*) Ah, yes, yes . . . (*With a sudden thought*) The Crabs are men. (*Pause.*) What? (*He sits down.*) Where did I discover that? (*Pause.*) I knew it . . . once . . . Yes, yes, yes. But I've got so much on my mind. (*Pause. In a decided tone*) Real men, good and handsome, on all the balconies of the centuries. When I was crawling in the yard, I thought I heard them saying: "What's that, brother?" And that . . . was me. (*He stands up, springs to attention, gives a military salute, and speaks in a loud voice.*) I, the Crab. (*He turns toward Johanna and speaks familiarly to her.*) Well, I said no, men won't judge my time. What will they be, after all? The sons of our sons. Are brats allowed to condemn their grandfathers? I turned the tables, and I cried: "Here is man; after me, the deluge; after the deluge, *you*, the Crabs!" All unmasked! The balconies swarming with Arthro-

pods. (*Solemnly*) You must know that the human
race started off on the wrong foot, but I put the lid
on its fabulous ill-fortune by handing over its mortal
remains to the Court of the Crustaceans. (*Pause. He
walks sideways slowly.*) Good. They will be men.
(*He laughs gently in an absent-minded way, and
walks backward toward the portrait of Hitler.*) Men,
you see that! (*Bristling suddenly*) Johanna, I challenge their competence. I take the matter out of their
hands, and I pass it over to you. Judge me.

JOHANNA (*more resigned than surprised*): *Judge* you?

FRANZ (*shouting*): Are you deaf? (*His violence gives
way to anxious surprise.*) What's that? (*He recovers
himself. With a dry, sinister, and almost conceited
laugh*) You shall judge me; by heaven, you shall
judge me.

JOHANNA: Only yesterday you were the witness—the
witness for mankind.

FRANZ: Yesterday was yesterday. (*He passes his hand
across his brow.*) The witness for mankind . . .
(*Laughing*) And who should that be? Come,
madame, it's mankind. A child could guess that. The
accused testifies for himself. I see that there is a
vicious circle. (*With somber pride*) I am mankind,
Johanna. I am every man and all mankind. I am the
century. (*A brief clownish humility*) Like anyone.

JOHANNA: In that case, I shall be trying someone else.

FRANZ: Who?

JOHANNA: Anyone.

FRANZ: The accused promises to be exemplary. I ought
to give evidence for the defense, but I'll indict
myself if you wish. (*Pause.*) Of course, you're free,
but if you abandon me without hearing me and for
fear of knowing me, you will have passed sentence in

any case. Decide. (*Pause. He points to the ceiling.*)
I tell them whatever comes into my head. Never
any reply. I tell them jokes and funny stories. I've
got to the point of wondering whether they swallow
them or whether they are holding them against me.
A pyramid of silence over my head. A silent mil-
lennium. That's killing me. And what if they don't
even know I exist? What if they have forgotten me?
What is to become of me without a trial? What
contempt! "You can do what you like; nobody cares!"
Well, don't I come into it? If a life is not sanctioned,
the earth consumes it. That was the Old Testament.
Here is the New. You shall be the future and the
present; the world and myself. Beyond you there is
nothing. You will make me forget the centuries. I
shall live. You will listen to me, and I shall surprise
your looks; I shall hear you reply to me. One day
perhaps, in years to come, you will recognize my
innocence, and I shall know it. What a day of
joyous celebration! You will be all to me, and all
will acquit me. (*Pause.*) Johanna, is it possible?
(*Pause.*)

JOHANNA: Yes.

FRANZ: Is it still possible to love me?

JOHANNA (*with a sad smile, but deeply sincere*): Un-
fortunately, yes.

(FRANZ *stands up. He appears relieved, almost happy.
He goes to* JOHANNA *and takes her in his arms.*)

FRANZ: I shall never be alone again. . . . (*He is about
to kiss her, then he suddenly breaks away and resumes his hard and wild manner.* JOHANNA *looks at
him, understands that he has again retreated into his
solitude, and she in turn hardens, with a bitter irony
turned only against herself.*) I beg your pardon,

Johanna; it's a little too soon to corrupt the judge
whom I have appointed over myself.

JOHANNA: I'm not your judge. One doesn't judge those
whom one loves.

FRANZ: And suppose you stop loving me? Won't that
be a judgment? The final judgment?

JOHANNA: How could I?

FRANZ: By learning who I am.

JOHANNA: I already know.

FRANZ (*rubbing his hands with a cheerful air*): Oh, no.
Not at all! Not at all! (*Pause. He looks quite mad.*)
A day will come, just like any other day. I shall talk
about myself, and you will listen. Then, suddenly,
love will be shattered. You will look at me with
horror, and I shall again become (*going down on
his hands and knees and walking sideways*) . . . a
crab.

JOHANNA (*looking at him in horror*): Stop!

FRANZ (*on his hands and knees*): You will look at me
with those eyes, exactly like that. (*He stands up
quickly.*) Condemned, eh? Condemned without right
of appeal. (*In a changed voice, ceremonious and
optimistic*) Of course, it is just as likely that I may
be acquitted.

JOHANNA (*tense and contemptuous*): I'm not sure that
you want to be.

FRANZ: Madame, I want to get it over with, one way
or the other. (*Pause.*)

JOHANNA: You've won. Bravo! If I go, I condemn you,
and if I stay, you sow mistrust between us. I can
already see it in your eyes. Well, let's get on with it.
Let's do our best to degrade ourselves together. Let's
take great pains to debase each other. We shall make
our love into an instrument of torture. We'll drink,

shall we? You'll go back to your champagne; mine was always whisky. I'll bring some. Both of us with a bottle, face to face and alone. (*With a bitter smile*) Do you know what we shall be, witness for mankind? A couple like any other couple. (*She pours herself some champagne and raises her glass.*) I drink to us. (*She drains the glass and throws it at the portrait of Hitler. The glass breaks as it hits the portrait. She takes an armchair from the heap of broken furniture, sets it up, and sits in it.*) Well?

FRANZ (*disconcerted*): Johanna . . . do you mean . . . ?

JOHANNA: I'm asking the questions. Well? What have you to say?

FRANZ: You haven't understood me. If it were only us, I swear . . .

JOHANNA: Who else is there?

FRANZ (*with an effort*): My sister Leni. If I decide to speak, it's to save us from her. I shall say . . . what there is to say without sparing myself—and in my own way, little by little. It will take months, years—it doesn't matter. I only ask you to trust me, and I shall trust you if you promise you'll believe no one but me.

JOHANNA (*looks at him for a time and speaks more gently*): Right. I'll believe only you.

FRANZ (*with a touch of solemnity, but sincerely*): So long as you keep that promise, Leni will have no power over us. (*He sits down.*) I was afraid. You were in my arms; I desired you. I was about to live . . . and all of a sudden I saw my sister, and I said to myself: "She'll smash us." (*He takes a handkerchief from his pocket and mops his brow.*) Whew! (*In a low voice*) It's summer, isn't it? It must be hot. (*Pause. He looks into space.*) Do you know that he has made me into a rather formidable machine?

JOHANNA: Your father?

FRANZ: Yes. A machine to give orders. (*A short laugh. Pause.*) Another summer, and the machine is still turning. Empty as usual. (*He stands up.*) I'll tell you my life, but don't expect any great villainies. Oh, no, not even that. Do you know why I reproach myself? I've done nothing. (*The light fades slowly.*) Nothing! Nothing! Never!

A WOMAN'S VOICE (*softly*): Soldier!

JOHANNA (*not hearing the woman*): You were in the war.

FRANZ: I was in it, all right.

(*The lights fade.*)

WOMAN'S VOICE (*louder*): Soldier!

(FRANZ *is standing downstage, and only he is visible.* JOHANNA, *seated in the armchair, is now in darkness.*)

FRANZ: It's not a matter of being in the war—it's what war does to us. While the fighting was on, I had a good laugh. I was a civilian in uniform. One night I became a soldier for good. (*He takes an officer's hat from the table behind him and places it on his head with a sharp movement.*) A poor tramp, defeated, useless. I was crossing Germany on the way back from Russia, hiding, and I came to a ruined village.

WOMAN'S VOICE (*louder, from the darkness*): Soldier!

FRANZ: What's that? (*He turns sharply. He has a flashlight in his left hand. With his right hand he draws his revolver from its holster. The flashlight is not burning.*) Who's calling me?

WOMAN: Take a look around.

FRANZ: How many are you?

WOMAN: There's nobody left up where you are. There's

just me, on the ground. (FRANZ *quickly turns on the flashlight and shines it on the floor. A woman in black is huddled against the wall, half lying on the floor.*) Put that out! You're blinding me. (FRANZ *turns off the flashlight. They can be seen in the diffused light that surrounds them.*) Ha! Ha! Shoot, then! Shoot! Finish your war by murdering a German woman!

(FRANZ *becomes aware that, without noticing it, he has trained his revolver on the woman. Horrified, he puts it back in its holster.*)

FRANZ: What are you doing there?

WOMAN: You can see—I'm up against the wall. (*Proudly*) It's my wall. The strongest one in the village—the only one left standing.

FRANZ: Come with me.

WOMAN: Turn on your flashlight. (*He turns it on, and the pool of light shows the floor. It reveals a blanket that covers the woman from head to foot.*) Look! (*She raises the blanket a little, and he shines the flashlight on what she is showing him, which is unseen by the audience. Then, with a grunt, he quickly switches off the flashlight.*) Yes, those were my legs.

FRANZ: What can I do for you?

WOMAN: Sit down a minute. (*He sits down near her.*) I've got one of our soldiers up against the wall. (*Pause.*) That's all I wanted. (*Pause.*) I was hoping that it would be my brother, but he was killed in Normandy. Never mind. You'll do. I would have said to him: "Look! (*Pointing to the ruins of the village*) That's your doing!"

FRANZ: His doing?

WOMAN (*speaking directly to* FRANZ): And yours, son.

FRANZ: Why?

WOMAN (*as though stating an obvious fact*): You let yourself be beaten.

FRANZ: Don't talk rubbish. (*He gets up quickly, facing the woman. He sees a poster, previously invisible, but now lighted by a spotlight. It is posted on the wall to the right of the woman, about six feet from the ground, and reads:* YOU ARE GUILTY!) Again! They've put them everywhere. (*He goes to tear it down.*)

WOMAN (*looking at him with her head thrown back*): Leave it! Leave it, I tell you! It's *my* wall. (FRANZ *draws back.*) You are guilty. (*She reads it and points to him.*) You, my brother, all of you.

FRANZ: You agree with what they say?

WOMAN: As night follows day. They're telling God that we're cannibals, and God listens to them because they have won. But I'll always believe that the real cannibal is the victor. Admit it, soldier; you didn't want to eat human flesh.

FRANZ (*wearily*): We've destroyed. Destroyed! Towns and villages! Capitals!

WOMAN: They've destroyed more. That's why they've beaten you. (FRANZ *shrugs his shoulders.*) Have you eaten human flesh?

FRANZ: What about your brother? Has he?

WOMAN: Not likely. He kept his good manners. Like you.

FRANZ (*after a pause*). Have they told you about the camps?

WOMAN: What camps?

FRANZ: You know very well—the extermination camps.

WOMAN: I've heard about them.

FRANZ: If you were told that your brother, when he

was killed, was a guard in one of those camps, would you be proud?

WOMAN (*fiercely*): Yes. Listen to me, my boy; if my brother had thousands of dead on his conscience, if among those dead there were women like me, children like those who are rotting under those stones there, I should be proud of him. I would know that he is in heaven and that he has the right to think: "I did what I could." But l know him. He loved us less than his honor, less than his virtues. That's it! (*Violently, with a sweeping gesture*) What we needed was a Terror—you should have wiped out everything.

FRANZ: We did.

WOMAN: Never enough. Not enough camps. Not enough executioners. You betrayed us by giving away what didn't belong to you. Every time you spared an enemy life, even in the cradle, you took one of ours. You wanted to fight without hatred, and you have infected me with the hatred that is eating out my heart. Where is your virtue, you poor soldier; you routed soldier, where is your honor? You are guilty. God won't judge you by your deeds, but by what you haven't dared to do—by the crimes that should have been committed and that you didn't commit. (*The lights have faded gradually, leaving only the poster visible. The voice continues, slowly dying away*) You are guilty! You are guilty! You! You!

(*The light fades from the poster, leaving the stage in complete darkness.*)

FRANZ (*in darkness*): Johanna!

(*The lights come on.* FRANZ *is standing bareheaded near the table.* JOHANNA *is seated in the armchair. The woman has disappeared.*)

JOHANNA (*with a start*): What?

(FRANZ *goes toward her. He looks at her steadily.*)

FRANZ: Johanna! (*He looks at her, trying to banish his memories.*)

JOHANNA (*drawing back rather coldly*): What happened to her?

FRANZ: The woman? That depends.

JOHANNA (*surprised*): On what?

FRANZ: My dreams.

JOHANNA: Wasn't it a memory?

FRANZ: It was also a dream. Sometimes I take her with me, sometimes I leave her there, and sometimes . . . In any case, she dies. It's a nightmare. (*He looks at her fixedly and talks to himself.*) I wonder whether I killed her.

JOHANNA (*not surprised, but with fear and disgust*): Ah! (*He laughs.*)

FRANZ (*with a gesture, as though pulling a trigger*): Like that. (*Smiling defiantly*) Would you have left her to suffer? There are crimes along all the roads. Prefabricated crimes that are only waiting for their criminals. The real soldier comes along and does the job. (*Sharply*) Don't you like history? I don't like your eyes. Ah! Finish her off any way you like. (*He strides away and turns near the table.*) "You are guilty!" What do you say? Was she right?

JOHANNA (*shrugging her shoulders*): She was mad.

FRANZ: Yes. What does that prove?

JOHANNA (*strong and clear*): We lost because we were short of men and planes!

FRANZ (*interrupting her*): I know! I know! That was Hitler's fault. (*Pause.*) I'm talking about myself. War was my lot—to what point should I have loved it? (*She wants to speak.*) Think! Think carefully! Your answer will be decisive.

JOHANNA (*ill at ease, annoyed, and hard*): I have thought.

FRANZ (*after a pause*): If indeed I had committed all the crimes that were condemned at Nuremberg . . .

JOHANNA: What crimes?

FRANZ: How should I know! Genocide and the whole works.

JOHANNA (*shrugging her shoulders*): Why should you have committed them?

FRANZ: Because war was my lot. When our fathers got our mothers pregnant, they made soldiers. I don't know why.

JOHANNA: A soldier is a man.

FRANZ: First, he is a soldier. Well? Would you still love me? (*She wants to speak.*) But take your time, for Christ's sake! (*She remains silent.*) Well?

JOHANNA: No.

FRANZ: You would no longer love me? (*She indicates no.*) Would I horrify you?

JOHANNA: Yes.

FRANZ (*bursting into laughter*): Good, good, good! Rest assured, Johanna, you're dealing with a virgin. Guaranteed innocence. (*She remains hard and challenging.*) You can have a good laugh at me. I killed Germany by being sentimental.

(*The door of the bathroom opens.* KLAGES *enters, closes the door, and goes slowly over to sit in* FRANZ's *chair. Neither* FRANZ *nor* JOHANNA *pays any attention to him.*)

FRANZ: There were five hundred of us near Smolensk. Holding on to a village. Major killed, captains killed, two of us left—two lieutenants—and a sergeant

major. A hell of a triumvirate. Lieutenant Klages
was a pastor's son, an idealist, up in the clouds.
Heinrich, the sergeant major, had his feet on the
ground, but he was one-hundred-per-cent Nazi. The
partisans had cut us off from the rear, and they had
the road under fire. Three days' rations left. We had
found two Russian peasants, locked them in a barn,
and given the prisoners a baptism.

KLAGES: What a brute!

FRANZ (*without turning around*): What?

KLAGES: Heinrich! I said: "What a brute!"

FRANZ (*vaguely, still without turning around*): Ah,
yes. . . .

KLAGES (*piteously, but with ominous undertones*):
Franz, I'm in a stinking mess. (FRANZ *turns quickly
toward him.*) The two peasants—he's determined to
make them talk.

FRANZ: Ah! (*Pause.*) And you don't want him to give
them the once-over?

KLAGES: Am I wrong?

FRANZ: That's not the question.

KLAGES: What is it, then?

FRANZ: Have you forbidden him to go into the barn?
(KLAGES *nods.*) Then he mustn't go in.

KLAGES: You know very well he'll take no notice of me.

FRANZ (*pretending indignation and astonishment*):
What?

KLAGES: I can't find the words.

FRANZ: What words?

KLAGES: The words to convince him.

FRANZ (*astounded*): You want him to be convinced as
well! (*Brutally*) Treat him like a dog. Make him
crawl!

KLAGES: I can't. If I despise a man, only one, even a

butcher, I'll never again have any respect for anyone.

FRANZ: If any subordinate, just one, refuses to obey you, you'll never again be obeyed by anyone. I couldn't care less about respect for man, but if you throw discipline to the winds, we'll be routed or massacred, or both.

KLAGES (*goes to the door, half opens it, and peeps through*): He's outside the barn. He's on the look-out. (*He closes the door and turns toward* FRANZ.) Let's spare them!

FRANZ: You will save them if you save your authority.

KLAGES: I thought . . .

FRANZ: What?

KLAGES: Heinrich listens to you as though you were God.

FRANZ: Because I treat him like dirt. It's understandable.

KLAGES (*embarrassed*): If the order came from you . . . (*Appealing*) Franz!

FRANZ: No. The prisoners come under you. If I gave an order instead of you, I would undermine you. And if I were to be killed in an hour, after having knocked the props from under you, Heinrich would take sole command. That would be a catastrophe for my men because he's stupid, and for your prisoners because he's vicious. (*He crosses the room and goes over to* JOHANNA.) Especially for Klages. Even though he was a lieutenant, Heinrich would have bumped him off.

JOHANNA: Why?

FRANZ: Klages hoped for our defeat.

KLAGES: I don't hope for it; I want it.

FRANZ: You have no right.

KLAGES: It'll be the end of Hitler.

FRANZ: And of Germany. (*Laughing*) Kaput! Kaput! (*Turning back to* JOHANNA) He was the champion of mental reservation. He condemned the Nazis in spirit to hide the fact that he was serving them in the flesh.

JOHANNA: He wasn't serving them.

FRANZ (*to* JOHANNA): Go on! You're just the same. His hands served them; his voice served them. He said to God: "I don't like what I'm doing." But he did it. (*Turning back to* KLAGES) You don't want anything to do with the war, and by refusing to take part, you condemn yourself to impotence. You've sold your soul for nothing, you moralist. I'll sell mine to some purpose. (*Pause.*) Win the war first, then we'll take care of Hitler.

KLAGES: It'll be too late then.

FRANZ: We'll see. (*Turning threateningly to* JOHANNA) I had been deceived, madame, and I had decided that I wouldn't be deceived again.

JOHANNA: Who deceived you?

FRANZ: You're asking me? Luther. (*Laughing*) See! Understand! I sent Luther to the devil, and I went off. War was my destiny, and I desired it with all my soul. I acted, at last. I interpreted the orders. I was at one with myself.

JOHANNA: To act means to kill?

FRANZ (*to* JOHANNA): That's acting. Writing one's name.

KLAGES: On what?

FRANZ (*to* KLAGES): On what's there. I write mine on those fields there. I'll take responsibility for the war as though I were carrying it on alone, and then, when I've won, I'll sign up again.

JOHANNA (*very abruptly*): What about the prisoners, Franz?

FRANZ (*turning to her*): Eh?

JOHANNA: You who take responsibility for everything—did you take responsibility for them?

FRANZ (*after a pause*): I got them out of it. (*To* KLAGES) How can I give him the order without undermining your authority? Wait a bit! (*He thinks.*) I know. (*He goes to the door, opens it, and calls out.*) Heinrich! (*He goes back to the table.* HEINRICH *runs in.*)

HEINRICH (*standing at attention and giving a military salute*): Here, lieutenant!

(*When he addresses* FRANZ, *his face breaks into a happy, confident, almost tender smile.* FRANZ *goes slowly over to him and inspects him from head to foot.*)

FRANZ: You're becoming careless, sergeant major. (*Pointing to a button that is hanging by a thread through a buttonhole*) What's this?

HEINRICH: It's . . . er . . . it's a button, lieutenant.

FRANZ (*good-naturedly*): You'll lose it, my friend. (*He pulls it off with a sudden jerk and holds it in his left hand.*) You'll sew it on.

HEINRICH (*disconsolate*): No one has any thread left, lieutenant.

FRANZ: You dare to answer back, you sack of shit! (*He slaps him hard on the face with his right hand.*) Pick it up! (*He drops the button. The sergeant major stoops to pick it up.*) Attention! (*The sergeant major picks up the button and springs to attention.*) Lieutenant Klages and I have decided to change duties every week, beginning today. In a moment you will escort him to the outposts. I'll take over his duties till Monday. Dismissed! (HEINRICH *gives a military salute.*) Wait! (*To* KLAGES) I believe there are some prisoners.

KLAGES: Two.

FRANZ: Very well. I'll take charge of them.

HEINRICH (*his eyes sparkling, believing that* FRANZ *will accept his suggestions*): Lieutenant.

FRANZ (*brutally, with an air of astonishment*): What?

HEINRICH: They're partisans.

FRANZ: Possibly. Well?

HEINRICH: If you would allow me . . .

KLAGES: I have already forbidden you to touch them.

FRANZ: You hear, Heinrich? That's an order. Get out!

KLAGES: Wait! Do you know what he said to me?

HEINRICH: I . . . I was joking, lieutenant.

FRANZ (*raising his eyebrows*): With a superior officer? (*To* KLAGES) What did he say to you?

KLAGES: "What will you do if I don't obey you?"

FRANZ (*coldly*): Oh! (*He turns to* HEINRICH.) I'll answer you now, sergeant major. If you don't obey . . . (*Tapping his holster*) I'll put a bullet through you.

(*Pause.*)

KLAGES (*to* HEINRICH): Escort me to the outposts.

(*He exchanges a wink with* FRANZ *and goes out behind* HEINRICH.)

FRANZ: Was it right to kill my soldiers?

JOHANNA: You didn't kill them.

FRANZ: I didn't do *everything* to stop them being killed.

JOHANNA: The prisoners wouldn't have talked.

FRANZ: How do you know?

JOHANNA: Peasants? They had nothing to tell.

FRANZ: Does that prove that they weren't partisans?

JOHANNA: Partisans don't usually talk.

FRANZ: Usually they didn't. (*Insistently, with an air of madness*) Germany is worth a crime, isn't she? (*Cynical, with an almost clownish offhandedness*) I don't know if I'm making myself understood. You are already another generation. (*Pause. Hard, violent, earnest, without looking at her, his eyes staring, standing almost at attention*) A short life with a first-class death. March! March! To the depths of horror. To hell and beyond! A powder magazine! I would have blown it up in the darkness. Everything would have gone up except my country. For a moment I would have been the cluster spinning above a mighty fireworks display, and then nothing more. The night and my name alone on the brass. (*Pause.*) Let's admit that I was reluctant. Principles, my dear, always principles. You can guess that I preferred my own soldiers to those two unknown prisoners. Nevertheless, I had to say no. Would that make me a cannibal? Pardon me, a vegetarian, rather. (*Pause. Pompously and in a legal manner*) He who does not do all does nothing. I did nothing. He who has done nothing is nobody. Nobody? (*Pointing to himself, as though answering a roll call.*) Present! (*Pause. To* JOHANNA) That's the most important point of the indictment.

JOHANNA: I acquit you.

FRANZ: I tell you, it must be debated.

JOHANNA: I love you.

FRANZ: Johanna! (*There is a knock at the landing door: five, four, then twice three. They look at each other.*) Well, it was a little late.

JOHANNA: Franz . . .

FRANZ: A little late to acquit me. (*Pause.*) Father has

talked. (*Pause.*) Johanna, you're going to witness an execution.

JOHANNA (*looking at him*): Yours? (*The knocking begins again.*) And will you allow yourself to be butchered? (*Pause.*) You don't love me, then?

FRANZ (*laughing silently*): I'll talk to you about our love in a moment . . . (*Pointing to the door*) . . . in front of her. It won't be nice. And remember this: I'll ask for your help, and you won't give it to me. (*Pause.*) If there's any chance left . . . Go in there! (*He pulls her to the bathroom, and she goes in. He closes the bathroom door, and then goes to open the landing door to* LENI. *He quickly takes off his wrist watch and puts it in his pocket.* LENI *comes in, carrying a plate with a small iced Savoy cake on it. There are four candles on the cake. She is carrying a newspaper under her left arm.*)

FRANZ: Why are you disturbing me at this time of day?

LENI: Do you know what time it is?

FRANZ: I know that you've only just left me.

LENI: Did it seem such a short time to you?

FRANZ: Yes. (*Pointing to the cake*) What's that?

LENI: A little cake. I would have given it to you to-morrow for your dessert.

FRANZ: Well?

LENI: You see, I'm bringing it to you this evening. With candles.

FRANZ: Why candles?

LENI: Count them.

FRANZ: One, two, three, four. Well?

LENI: You're thirty-four.

FRANZ: I was—on February the fifteenth.

LENI: The fifteenth of February was a birthday.

FRANZ: And what's today?

LENI: A date.

FRANZ: Good. (*He takes the cake and carries it to the table.*) "Franz!" Was it you who wrote my name?

LENI: Who else?

FRANZ: Fame! (*He looks at his name.*) "Franz" in pink icing. Prettier and more flattering than brass. (*He lights the candles.*) Burn slowly, candles. As you burn out, so will I. (*Casually*) Have you seen father?

LENI: He came to see me.

FRANZ: In your room.

LENI: Yes.

FRANZ: Did he stay long?

LENI: Long enough.

FRANZ: In your room. That's a special favor.

LENI: I'll pay for it.

FRANZ: So will I.

LENI: You will.

FRANZ (*cutting the cake in two*): This is my body. (*Pouring champagne into two glasses*) This is my blood. (*Handing the cake to* LENI) Help yourself. (*She smiles and shakes her head.*) Poisoned?

LENI: Why should it be?

FRANZ: You're right. Why? (*He offers her a glass.*) Will you drink a toast? (LENI *takes the glass and looks at it suspiciously.*) A crab?

LENI: Lipstick. (*He takes the glass from her and smashes it against the table.*)

FRANZ: It's yours. You didn't wash it properly. (*He offers her the filled glass. She takes it. He pours champagne into a third glass for himself.*) Drink to me!

LENI: To you! (*She raises her glass.*)

FRANZ: To me! (*He clinks his glass against hers.*) What do you wish me?

LENI: That nothing should happen.

FRANZ: Nothing? Oh! Anything else? An excellent idea. (*Raising his glass*) I drink to nothing. (*He drinks and puts down his glass.* LENI *sways, and he catches her in his arms and leads her to the armchair.*) Sit down, little sister.

LENI (*sitting down*): Excuse me, I'm tired. (*Pause.*) And the hardest part is still to come.

FRANZ: You're right. (*He mops his brow.*)

LENI (*as though to herself*): I'm freezing. Another rotten summer.

FRANZ (*amazed*): It's stifling.

LENI (*agreeably*): Is it? Perhaps it is. (*She looks at him.*)

FRANZ: Why are you looking at me like that?

LENI (*after a pause*): You've changed. It should show.

FRANZ: Doesn't it, then?

LENI: No, I see *you*. It's deceptive. (*Pause.*) It's no one's fault, my dear. You should have loved me, but I suppose you couldn't.

FRANZ: I loved you a lot.

LENI (*violently angry*): Be quiet! (*She masters herself, but to the end her voice remains very hard.*) Father tells me that you've met our sister-in-law.

FRANZ: She comes to see me occasionally. A very nice girl. I'm pleased for Werner's sake. What was it you told me? She isn't a hunchback.

LENI: She is.

FRANZ: She isn't. (*Drawing a line down with his hand*) She's . . .

LENI: Her back is straight enough, but that doesn't mean she isn't a hunchback. (*Pause.*) Do you think she's beautiful?

FRANZ: Do you?

LENI: Beautiful as death.

FRANZ: It's funny you should say that. I thought the same myself.

LENI: I drink to her! (*She empties her glass and throws it away.*)

FRANZ (*casually*): Are you jealous?

LENI: I feel nothing.

FRANZ: No, it's too soon.

LENI: Much too soon. (*Pause.* FRANZ *takes a piece of cake and eats it. He points to the cake and laughs.*)

FRANZ: A gag for the rascal, eh? (*He holds his piece of cake in his left hand while he opens the drawer, takes out the revolver, and—still eating the cake— hands it to* LENI.) Here!

LENI: What should I do with it?

FRANZ (*showing her*): Shoot. And leave her alone.

LENI (*laughing*): Put it back in the drawer. I don't even know how to use it.

FRANZ (*still holding the revolver on the palm of his outstretched hand*): You won't harm her?

LENI: Have I looked after her for thirteen years? Have I begged for her caresses? Swallowed her insults? Have I fed her, washed her, clothed her, defended her against everyone? She owes me nothing, and I won't touch her. I want her to suffer a little, but only because of my love for you.

FRANZ (*a statement rather than a question*): Do I owe everything to you?

LENI (*fiercely*): Everything!

FRANZ (*pointing to the revolver*): Take it, then.

LENI: You'd love me to. What a memory you would
leave her! And wouldn't she make a fine widow! She's
cut out for it. (*Pause.*) I'm not thinking of killing
you, my love, and there's nothing in the world I
fear more than your death. Only I'm obliged to hurt
you deeply. I intend to tell Johanna everything.

FRANZ: Everything?

LENI: Everything. I'll shatter her love for you. (FRANZ's
hand tightens on the revolver.) Go on, shoot your
poor sister. I've written a letter; in case of an accident, Johanna will get it this evening. (*Pause.*) Do
you think I'm getting revenge?

FRANZ: Aren't you?

LENI: I'm doing what's right. Dead or alive, it's right
that you should belong to me, for I'm the only one
who loves you as you are.

FRANZ: The only one? (*Pause.*) Yesterday I would have
committed murder. Today I see a gleam of hope.
One chance in a hundred that she'll accept me. (*Re-
placing the revolver in the drawer*) If you're still
alive, Leni, it's because I've decided to play this
chance to the end.

LENI: Very well, let her know what I know, and we'll
see who wins. (*She stands up and goes to the bathroom door. In passing behind him, she throws the
newspaper on the table.* FRANZ *starts.*)

FRANZ: What's that?

LENI: The *Frankfurter Zeitung.* There's an article
about us.

FRANZ: You and me?

LENI: The family. They're doing a series: "The Giants
Who Have Rebuilt Germany." Honor where it's
due. They start with the Gerlachs.

FRANZ (*undecided whether or not to take the news-paper*): Is father a giant?

LENI (*pointing to the article*): That's what they say. Just read it. They say he's the greatest of the lot. (FRANZ *picks up the paper with a kind of hoarse growl and opens it. He is seated facing the audience, with his back to the bathroom, his head hidden by the opened paper.* LENI *knocks on the bathroom door.*)

LENI: Open up! I know you're there.

JOHANNA (*opening the door*): All right. I don't like hiding. (*In friendly tone*) Hello!

LENI (*likewise*): Hello!

(JOHANNA, *worried, pushes past* LENI *and goes straight to* FRANZ. *She looks at him as he is reading.*)

JOHANNA: Newspapers? (FRANZ *does not even turn around. She turns to* LENI.) You're moving fast.

LENI: I'm in a hurry.

JOHANNA: In a hurry to kill him?

LENI (*shrugging her shoulders*): Of course not.

JOHANNA: Run! We've beaten you to it. From today I'm sure he'll be able to bear the truth.

LENI: That's funny. He's also sure that you'll be able to bear the truth.

JOHANNA (*smiling*): I'll bear anything. Did your father tell you?

LENI: Yes, he did.

JOHANNA: He threatened that he would. It was he who told me how to get in here.

LENI: Oh!

JOHANNA: Didn't he tell you that?

LENI: No.

JOHANNA: He's using us.

LENI: So it seems.

JOHANNA: And you don't mind?

LENI: No.

JOHANNA: What do you want?

LENI (*pointing to* FRANZ): I want you to get out of his life.

JOHANNA: I never will.

LENI: I'll make you.

JOHANNA: Try! (*Pause.*)

FRANZ (*puts down the paper, gets up, and goes right up to* JOHANNA): You promised to believe only me, Johanna. This is the time to remind you of your promise. Today our love depends completely on that.

JOHANNA: I shall believe only you. (*They look at each other. She smiles at him tenderly and confidently, but* FRANZ's *face is pale and twitching. He forces a smile, turns, goes back to his seat, and picks up his paper again.*) Well, Leni?

LENI: There are two of us. One too many. We'll see which one it is.

JOHANNA: How?

LENI: We need a real test. If you win, you'll take my place.

JOHANNA: You'll cheat.

LENI: I don't need to.

JOHANNA: Why?

LENI: You're sure to lose.

JOHANNA: Let's have the test.

LENI: Right! (*Pause.*) Has he told you about Sergeant Major Heinrich and some Russian prisoners? Did he accuse himself of condemning his comrades to death by saving the life of two partisans?

JOHANNA: Yes.

LENI: And did you tell him he was right?

JOHANNA (*sarcastically*): You know everything.

LENI: Don't be surprised. He tried it on me.

JOHANNA: Well? Are you suggesting that he lied?

LENI: Nothing he told you was untrue.

JOHANNA: But . . .

LENI: But that's not the end of the story. That's the test, Johanna.

FRANZ: Terrific! (*He throws the paper on the table and gets up, his face pale, madness in his eyes.*) A hundred and twenty slipways! The total distance covered by our ships every year would reach from here to the moon. Germany is on her feet. Long live Germany! (*He goes toward* LENI *with mechanical strides.*) Thank you, sister. Now leave us alone.

LENI: No.

FRANZ (*shouting, commandingly*): I said leave us alone. (*He tries to pull her toward the door.*)

JOHANNA: Franz!

FRANZ: What?

JOHANNA: I want to know the end of the story.

FRANZ: It has no end. Everybody was killed except me.

LENI: Look at him. One day in forty-nine he admitted everything to me.

JOHANNA: Admitted what?

FRANZ: That's all made up. How can one talk seriously to her? I was joking! (*Pause.*) Johanna, you promised to believe no one but me.

JOHANNA: Yes.

FRANZ: Believe me. Good God, believe me, then!

JOHANNA: I . . . You're not the same when she's here. (LENI *laughs.*) Make me want to believe you. Tell me she's lying. Speak! You didn't do anything, did you?

FRANZ (*almost a groan*): Nothing.

JOHANNA (*urgently*): But say it. I must hear you. Say: "I didn't do anything."

FRANZ (*in a distraught voice*): I didn't do anything.

JOHANNA (*looking at him in a kind of terror, cries out*): Ha! (*She stifles her cry.*) I no longer recognize you.

FRANZ (*stubbornly*): I didn't do anything.

LENI: But you let someone else do it.

JOHANNA: Who?

LENI: Heinrich.

JOHANNA: The two prisoners . . . ?

LENI: Those two to begin with.

JOHANNA: Were there others?

LENI: After the first time you lose your scruples.

FRANZ: I'll explain. I lose my head when I see the two of you. You're killing me. . . . Johanna, when we're alone . . . Everything has happened so quickly. . . . But I'll be able to explain. It'll all come back. I'll tell you the whole truth. Johanna, I love you more than my life. . . . (*He takes her by the arm, but she tears herself free, shouting at him.*)

JOHANNA: Let me go! (*She stands alongside* LENI. FRANZ *stands bewildered in front of her.*)

LENI (*to* JOHANNA): The test came off badly.

JOHANNA: I lost. Keep him.

FRANZ (*distracted*): Listen to me, both of you. . . .

JOHANNA (*with hatred*): You were a torturer! You!

FRANZ: Johanna! (*She looks at him*). Not with those eyes! No. Not with those eyes! (*Pause.*) I knew it. (*He bursts out laughing and goes down on his hands and knees.*) Back we go! (LENI *cries out. He stands up.*) You've never seen me as a crab, little sister? (*Pause.*) Get out, both of you! (LENI *goes to the table, intending to open the drawer.*) Ten past five.

Tell father I'll meet him at six o'clock in the conference room. Get out! (*A long silence. The lights begin to fade.* JOHANNA *goes out first, without looking back.* LENI *hesitates a little, then follows her.* FRANZ *sits down and picks up the paper.*) A hundred and twenty slipways! An empire!

CURTAIN

ACT V

The same décor as Act One. It is six o'clock. Daylight
is fading, but this is not at first apparent because the
shutters of the French windows are closed. The room
is in semi-darkness. The clock strikes six. On the third
stroke the shutter of the left-hand French window is
opened from the outside, and the light streams in.
The FATHER pushes the French window open and
enters. At the same time FRANZ's door opens and
FRANZ appears on the landing. The two men look at
each other for a moment. FRANZ is carrying in his
hand a small square black case—his tape recorder.

FRANZ (without moving): Hello, father.
FATHER (in a natural and familiar voice): Hello, son.
  (He sways for a moment and steadies himself against
  the back of a chair.)
FATHER: Wait! I'll let some light in.
  (He opens the other French window and pushes
  back the other shutter. A green light, as at the end of
  Act One, streams into the room.)
FRANZ (descending one step): I'm listening.
FATHER: I've nothing to say to you.
FRANZ: What? You bother Leni with requests. . . .
FATHER: My boy, I've come to this lodge because you
  asked me to come.
FRANZ (looking at his father in amazement, then break-
  ing into a laugh): That's true, I admit. (He comes
  down one more step, then stops.) A fine game. You

played off Johanna against Leni, then Leni against Johanna. Mate in three.

FATHER: Who is checkmate?

FRANZ: Me—the black king. Aren't you tired of winning?

FATHER: I'm tired of everything, my son, except that. One never wins. I'm trying to hedge my bet.

FRANZ (*shrugging his shoulders*): You always end up by doing what you want.

FATHER: That's the surest way of losing.

FRANZ (*bitterly*): Perhaps so. (*Sharply*) What *do* you want?

FATHER: Now? To see you.

FRANZ: Well, here I am! Take a good look at me while you still can. I've reserved some very choice news for you. (*The* FATHER *coughs.*) Don't cough.

FATHER (*with a touch of humility*): I'll try. (*He coughs again.*) It's not very easy. . . . (*Regaining control of himself*) There!

FRANZ (*slowly, looking at his* FATHER): How sad you look. (*Pause.*) Come on, smile! It's a celebration. Father and son reunited. Kill the fatted calf. (*Suddenly*) You won't be my judge.

FATHER: Who's talking of that?

FRANZ: It's in your eyes. (*Pause.*) Two criminals. One condemns the other in the name of principles they have both violated. What do you call that farce?

FATHER (*calmly and without expression*): Justice. (*A short pause.*) Are you a criminal?

FRANZ: Yes. So are you. (*Pause.*) I don't accept your competence to judge me.

FATHER: Then why did you want to speak to me?

FRANZ: To tell you I've lost everything, and you'll lose everything. (*Pause.*) Swear on the Bible that you will not judge me! Swear, or I'll go straight back into my room.

FATHER (*going to the Bible and placing his hand on it*): I swear!

FRANZ: All right! (*He comes down and places his tape recorder on the table. He turns, and father and son are face to face on the same level.*) Where are the years? You're still the same.

FATHER: No.

FRANZ (*approaching him as though fascinated. With a marked insolence, but defensive*): I feel nothing at seeing you again. (*Pause. With an almost involuntary movement he places his hand on his father's arm.*) Old Hindenburg, eh? (*He draws back, speaking harshly*) I'm a torturer. (*Silence. He shouts*) Do you hear?

FATHER (*with no change of expression*): Yes. Go on.

FRANZ: That's all. We were being harassed by partisans, and the village was in league with them. I tried to make two villagers talk. (*Pause. Abruptly and nervously*) The same old story.

FATHER (*heavily and slowly, but with no expression*): The same.

(*Pause.* FRANZ *looks at him disdainfully.*)

FRANZ: I think you're judging me, aren't you?

FATHER: No.

FRANZ: You'd better not. My dear father, let's be clear on this: it's because you're an informer that I'm a torturer.

FATHER: I didn't inform on anyone.

FRANZ: What about the Polish rabbi?

FATHER: Not even him. I took some . . . unpleasant risks.

FRANZ: I'll say no more. (*Thinking of the past*) Un-

pleasant risks? So did I. (*Laughing*) Oh, very unpleasant. (*He laughs. The* FATHER *takes advantage of
this to cough.*) What's the matter?

FATHER: I'm laughing with you.

FRANZ: You're coughing. Stop, for God's sake. You're
rasping my throat.

FATHER: Forgive me.

FRANZ: Are you going to die?

FATHER: You know I am.

FRANZ (*starting forward, then quickly jumping back*):
Good riddance! (*His hands tremble.*) That must hurt
like hell.

FATHER: What?

FRANZ: That damned cough.

FATHER (*annoyed*): No, it doesn't. (*He has another
fit of coughing, then calms down.*)

FRANZ: I feel your pain. (*Staring at him*) I lacked
imagination.

FATHER: When?

FRANZ: Out there. (*A long silence. He turns from his
FATHER and looks toward the door upstage. When he
speaks, he sees his past, except when he speaks
directly to his FATHER.*) The superior officers wiped
out. The sergeant major and Klages at my beck and
call. The soldiers at my mercy. Only one order: hold
on! I hold on. I choose the living and the dead. You
go and get yourself killed! You, stay here! (*Pause. He
comes downstage, proud and sinister.*) I have supreme
power. (*Pause.*) What? (*He seems to be listening
to an invisible questioner, then he turns to his
FATHER.*) Someone kept asking me: "What will you
do with it?"

FATHER: Who?

FRANZ: It was in the night air. Every night. (*Imitat-*

ing the whispering of unknown questioners) What
will you do with it? What will you do with it?
(*Shouting*) Idiots! I'll go right through with it.
Right to the limits of my power. (*Quickly, to his*
FATHER) Do you know why?

FATHER: Yes.

FRANZ (*rather disconcerted*): Oh?

FATHER: For once in your life you were powerless.

FRANZ (*loudly, laughing*): Old Hindenburg is no fool.
Good old Hindenburg! Yes, I was. (*He stops laughing.*) Here, and because of you. You handed the
rabbi over to them. Four of them held me down
while the others beat him to death. What could I do?
(*Lifting the little finger of his left hand and looking
at his* FATHER) Not even raise my little finger.
(*Pause.*) A curious experience, but I wouldn't recom-
mend it for future leaders. You never get over it. You
made me a prince, father. And do you know who
made me a king?

FATHER: Hitler.

FRANZ: Yes; through shame. After that . . . incident,
power became my vocation. Do you know also that
I admired him?

FATHER: Hitler?

FRANZ: Didn't you know? Oh, I hated him, before and
after. But that day he possessed me. Two leaders—
either they have to kill each other, or one becomes
the other's wife. I was Hitler's wife. The rabbi was
bleeding, and I discovered at the heart of my
powerlessness some strange kind of approval. (*He is
back again in the past.*) I have supreme power.
Hitler has changed me, made me implacable and
sacred, made me himself. I am Hitler, and I shall surpass myself. (*Pause. To the* FATHER) No rations

left. My soldiers were prowling around the barn. (*Back in the past*) Four good Germans will crush me to the earth, and my own men will bleed the prisoners to death. No! I shall never again fall into abject powerlessness. I swear it. It's dark. Horror has not yet been let loose. . . . I'll grab them quickly. If anyone lets it loose, it will be me. I'll assume the evil; I'll display my power by the singularity of an unforgettable act; change *living* men into vermin. I alone will deal with the prisoners. I'll debase them into abject wretches. They'll talk. Power is an abyss, and I see its depths. It is not enough to choose who shall live and who shall die. I shall decide life or death with a penknife and a cigarette lighter. (*Distractedly*) Fascinating! It is the glory of kings to go to hell. I shall go there. (*He stands as though in a trance, downstage.*)

FATHER (*in a matter-of-fact voice*): Did they talk?

FRANZ (*rudely awakened from his memories*): What's that? (*Pause.*) No. (*Pause.*) They died without talking.

FATHER: Loser wins.

FRANZ: Eh! Everything has to be learned. I hadn't the knack . . . then.

FATHER (*with a sad smile*): Nevertheless, it was they who decided life or death.

FRANZ (*shouting*): I'd have done the same. I would have died under the blows without saying a word. (*He calms down.*) So, what the hell; I kept my authority.

FATHER: How long?

FRANZ: Ten days. Ten days later enemy tanks attacked, and we were all dead—including the prisoners. (*Laughing*) I beg your pardon. Except me! I wasn't killed. Not in the least. (*Pause.*) I'm not sure about anything I've told you—except that I tortured them.

FATHER: And then what? (FRANZ *shrugs his shoulders.*) You kept on walking? You hid? Then you came home?

FRANZ. Yes. (*Pause.*) The ruins gave me my justification; I loved our looted houses and our mutilated children. I pretended that I was locking myself up so that I shouldn't witness Germany's agony. It's a lie. I wanted my country to die, and I shut myself up so that I shouldn't be a witness to its resurrection. (*Pause.*) Judge me!

FATHER: You made me swear on the Bible. . . .

FRANZ: I've changed my mind. Let's get it over with.

FATHER: No.

FRANZ: I tell you, I release you from your oath.

FATHER: Would the torturer accept the verdict of the informer?

FRANZ: There isn't a God, is there?

FATHER: I'm afraid there isn't. It's rather a nuisance at times.

FRANZ: Then, informer or no informer, you're my natural judge. (*Pause. The* FATHER *shakes his head.*) Won't you judge me? Not at all? Then you've something else in mind. Something worse. (*Sharply*) You're waiting. What for?

FATHER: Nothing. You're here.

FRANZ: You're waiting. I know your long, long waits. I've seen you facing real hard cases, real scoundrels. They'd insult you, and you'd say nothing; you would wait. And in the end they'd dissolve. (*Pause.*) Speak! Speak! Say anything! I can't stand it.

(*Pause.*)

FATHER: What are you going to do?

FRANZ: I'm going back up there.

FATHER: When will you come down again?

FRANZ: Never.

FATHER: Won't you see anyone?

FRANZ: I'll see Leni—for what I need.

FATHER: And Johanna?

FRANZ (*curtly*): Finished. (*Pause.*) She had no guts, that girl. . . .

FATHER: Were you in love with her?

FRANZ: The loneliness was getting me down. (*Pause.*) If she had accepted me as I am . . .

FATHER: And do you accept yourself?

FRANZ: What about you? Do you accept me?

FATHER: No.

FRANZ (*deeply hurt*): Not even a father.

FATHER: Not even a father.

FRANZ (*in a changed voice*): Well? What the hell are we doing together? (*The* FATHER *does not reply, and* FRANZ *continues in a voice of deep anguish.*) Ah, I should never have agreed to see you again. I knew it. I knew it.

FATHER: Knew what?

FRANZ: What would happen to me.

FATHER: Nothing is happening to you.

FRANZ: Not yet; but you're there and I'm here, as in my dreams. And you're waiting, as in my dreams. (*Pause.*) Very well, I can wait too. (*Pointing to the door of his room*) I'll put that door between us. Six months of patience. (*He points to his father's head.*) In six months that skull will be empty, those eyes will no longer see; the worms will be eating those lips and the contempt written on them.

FATHER: I have no contempt for you.

FRANZ (*sarcastically*): Really? After what I've told you?

FATHER: You've told me nothing.

FRANZ (*stunned*): What do you mean?

FATHER: I've known about your Smolensk business for three years.

FRANZ (*violently*): Impossible! Dead! No witnesses! Dead and buried! All of them!

FATHER: Except two, whom the Russians released. They came to see me. It was in March fifty-six. Ferist and Scheidemann. You remember them?

FRANZ (*taken aback*): No. (*Pause.*) What did they want?

FATHER: Money, to keep their mouths shut.

FRANZ: Well?

FATHER: I don't fall for blackmail.

FRANZ: And they?

FATHER: Not a word. You had forgotten them. Go on.

FRANZ (*looking into space*): Three years ago?

FATHER: Three years. I announced your death almost immediately, and the following year I sent for Werner. It was the wisest thing.

FRANZ (*who has not been listening*): Three years! I was making speeches to the Crabs. I was lying to them. And down here I had been found out for three years. (*Suddenly*) It was from that time that you wanted to see me, wasn't it?

FATHER: Yes.

FRANZ: Why?

FATHER (*shrugging his shoulders*): I wanted to.

FRANZ: They were sitting in your office, and you were listening to them because they had known me. And then, at a certain point, one of them said: "Franz von Gerlach is a butcher." Sensation! (*Trying to joke*) I hope you were very surprised.

FATHER: No. Not very.

FRANZ (*crying out*): I was clean when I left you. I was
pure. I wanted to save the Pole. . . . You weren't
surprised? (*Pause.*) What did you think? You knew
nothing till then, and suddenly you knew everything! (*Shouting louder*) For God's sake what did you
think?

FATHER (*with deep tenderness*): My poor boy!

FRANZ: What?

FATHER: You ask me what I thought, and I'm telling
you. (*Pause.* FRANZ *stands up straight, then he col-
lapses, sobbing, on his* FATHER's *shoulder.*) My poor
boy! (*He awkwardly caresses the back of* FRANZ's
neck.) My poor boy!
(*Pause.*)

FRANZ (*suddenly jumping up*): Stop! (*Pause.*)It's the
effect of the shock. I haven't cried for sixteen years,
and I won't do it again for another sixteen. Don't
pity me; it makes me want to bite. (*Pause.*) I don't
love myself very much.

FATHER: Why should you love yourself?

FRANZ: You're right there.

FATHER: That's my concern.

FRANZ: You love me! You? You love the butcher of
Smolensk?

FATHER: The butcher of Smolensk is you, my son.

FRANZ: All right, all right, don't let it disturb you.
(*With a deliberately coarse laugh*) It takes all kinds
to make a world. (*Suddenly*) You're using me.
When you show your feelings, it's because it suits
your plans. I say you're using me. A few hard knocks,
and then one goes soft. When you think you've got
me where you want me . . . Come on! You've had
plenty of time to think about this affair, and you're

too domineering not to want to settle it your own
way.

FATHER (*deeply ironical*): Domineering! I've got over
that. (*Pause. He laughs to himself, grimly amused,
then turns to* FRANZ, *speaking softly, but firmly*) As
for that business, I'll settle it.

FRANZ (*jumping back*): I'll stop you. Is it any concern
of yours?

FATHER: I don't want you to suffer any more.

FRANZ (*hard and brutal, as though accusing someone
other than himself*): I'm not suffering; I made others
suffer. Perhaps you see the distinction.

FATHER: I do.

FRANZ: I've forgotten everything. Even their cries. I'm
empty.

FATHER: I expect so. But it's even harder, isn't it?

FRANZ: Why should you care?

FATHER: For fourteen years you have been a prey to
suffering that you created and that you don't feel.

FRANZ: Who's asking you to talk about me? Yes, it's
even harder. I am its horse, and it rides me. I
wouldn't wish you to carry such a rider. (*Suddenly*)
Well? What's the solution? (*He looks at his* FATHER;
his eyes staring) Go to the devil! (*He turns his back
to him and climbs the stairs slowly and painfully.
The* FATHER *makes no attempt to stop him until he
has reached the landing.*)

FATHER (*in a loud voice*): Germany is in your room!
(FRANZ *turns slowly.*) She's alive, Franz! You'll never
forget her again!

FRANZ: She's struggling along, I know, in spite of her
defeat. I'll put up with it.

FATHER: As a result of her defeat, she's the greatest
power in Europe. Will you put up with that? (*Pause.*)

We're the apple of discord and the prize at stake. They pander to us. All markets are open to us, and our machines are going full blast. We're a foundry. A lucky defeat, Franz. We have guns and butter. And soldiers, son. Tomorrow the bomb! Then we shall toss our mane, and you'll see our patrons jump like fleas.

FRANZ (*in a last defense*): We're beaten, and we dominate Europe! What should we have done if we had won?

FATHER: We couldn't have won.

FRANZ: Did we have to lose the war, then?

FATHER: We had to play loser wins—as always.

FRANZ: Is that what you did?

FATHER: Yes. From the opening of hostilities.

FRANZ: And those who loved their country enough to sacrifice their military honor for victory . . .

FATHER (*in a hard, level voice*): Risked prolonging the massacre and hindering reconstruction. (*Pause.*) The truth is that they did nothing at all except commit individual murders.

FRANZ: A fine subject for meditation. Something for me to think about in my room.

FATHER: You won't stay there a minute longer.

FRANZ: That's where you're wrong. I'll deny this country that rejects me.

FATHER: You have tried for thirteen years without much success. Now could you go back to that game you've been playing?

FRANZ: How could I drop it? Either Germany must die or I shall become a common criminal.

FATHER: Precisely.

FRANZ (*quickly, looking at his* FATHER): Well? I don't want to die.

FATHER (*calmly*): Why not?

FRANZ: You may well ask. You've made your name.

FATHER: If you knew how little I care.

FRANZ: You're lying, father. You wanted to build ships, and you built them.

FATHER: I built them for you.

FRANZ: What! I thought you made me for them. At any rate, they are there. When you're dead, you'll be a fleet. What about me? What will I leave behind?

FATHER: Nothing.

FRANZ (*wildly*): That's why I shall live to a hundred. I have only my life. (*Overwrought*) That's all I have. They won't take it from me. Believe me, I hate it, but I prefer it to *nothing*.

FATHER: Both your life and your death are merely *nothing*. You are nothing, you do nothing, you have done nothing, and you can do nothing. (*A long pause. The* FATHER *goes slowly over to the stairs, leans against the banister, and looks up at* FRANZ.) Forgive me.

FRANZ (*stiffening in fear*): Me forgive you? It's a trick! (*The* FATHER *waits. Suddenly*) Forgive you for what?

FATHER: For you. (*Pause. He smiles.*) Parents are idiots. They stop the sun. I thought the world would never change. It has changed. Do you remember that future I had mapped out for you?

FRANZ: Yes.

FATHER: I was always talking to you about it, and you could see it. (FRANZ *nods assent.*) Well, it was my own past.

FRANZ: Yes.

FATHER: You knew?

FRANZ: I always knew. At first I liked it.

FATHER: My poor boy! I wanted you to run the firm after me. But it does the running. It chooses its own men. It has got rid of me. I own it, but I no longer run it. And you, little prince, it rejected you from the start. What does it need with a prince? It trains and recruits its own managers. (FRANZ *comes slowly downstairs while his father is speaking.*) I had given you all the talents and my bitter taste for power, but it was no use. What a pity! In order to act, you took the greatest risks and, you see, the firm turned all your acts into gestures. In the end, your torment drove you to crime, and because of that very crime it casts you out. It fattens on your defeat. I don't like regrets, Franz. They serve no purpose. If I could believe that you might be useful somewhere else, and in some other sphere . . . but I made you a monarch, and today that means good-for-nothing.

FRANZ (*with a smile*): Was I destined . . . ?

FATHER: Yes.

FRANZ: To impotence?

FATHER: Yes.

FRANZ: To crime?

FATHER: Yes.

FRANZ: By you?

FATHER: By my passions, which I implanted in you. Tell your Court of Crabs that I alone am guilty— of everything.

FRANZ (*smiling again*): That's what I wanted to hear you say. (*He comes down the stairs to the same level as his* FATHER.) Well, I accept.

FATHER: What?

FRANZ. What you expect of me. (*Pause.*) On one condition: that it is both of us, and at once.

FATHER (*taken aback*): At once?

FRANZ: Yes.

FATHER (*huskily*): Do you mean today?

FRANZ: I mean this very moment. (*Pause.*) Isn't that what you wanted?

FATHER (*coughs*): Not . . . so soon.

FRANZ: Why not?

FATHER: I have just found you again.

FRANZ: You have found *no one*. Not even yourself. (*He is calm and straightforward for the first time, but completely despairing.*) I shall only have been one of your images. The others have remained in your head. As luck would have it, this is the one that became incarnate. In Smolensk one night it had . . . what? A moment of independence. So you are guilty of everything except that. (*Pause.*) I lived for thirteen years with a loaded revolver in my drawer. Do you know why I didn't kill myself? I said to myself: "What's done is done." (*Pause. With deep sincerity*) Dying won't settle anything. That won't settle anything for me. I wished—you will laugh—I wished that I had never been born. I didn't always lie to myself up there. In the evenings I used to walk up and down the room and think of you.

FATHER: I was here, in this armchair. You walked; I listened.

FRANZ (*indifferent and unmoved*): Oh? (*Continuing*) I used to think: if only he could find a way of recapturing that rebel image, of putting it back into me so that it reabsorbs me, then there would never have been anything but him.

FATHER: Franz, there never has been anything but me.

FRANZ: That's easily said. Prove it. (*Pause.*) While we live, we shall be two. (*Pause.*) The Mercedes was a

six-seater, but you only used to take me in it. You
would say: "Franz, we must toughen you up for war.
We will go really fast." I was eight. We took the
road along the Elbe. . . . Is the Teufelsbrücke still
there?

FATHER: Yes.

FRANZ: A dangerous road. There were deaths there
every year.

FATHER: There are even more every year now.

FRANZ: You would say: "Here we go!" as you stepped
on the accelerator. I was wild with fear and joy.

FATHER (*smiling lightly*): We almost capsized once.

FRANZ: Twice. Cars go much faster these days, don't
they?

FATHER: Your sister's Porsche does a hundred and
twelve miles' an hour.

FRANZ: Let's take it.

FATHER: So soon! . . .

FRANZ: What are you hoping for?

FATHER: A respite.

FRANZ: You're having it. (*Pause.*) You know very well
that it will not last. (*Pause.*) Within an hour I
would hate you.

FATHER: Don't you now?

FRANZ: At this moment, no. (*Pause.*) Your image will
be shattered together with all those that never left
your head. You will be my cause and my fate, right
to the end.

(*Pause.*)

FATHER: Very well. (*Pause.*) I made you. I will unmake
you. My death will envelop yours, and in the end I
shall be the only one to die. (*Pause.*) Wait. I did
not think it would go so fast for me either. (*With
a smile that barely hides his anguish*) It's funny, a

life that goes up in smoke. That . . . that means nothing. (*Pause.*) I shall not be judged. (*Pause.*) You know, I didn't like myself either.

FRANZ (*placing his hand on his* FATHER'S *arm*): That was my concern.

FATHER (*the same anguished smile*): Well, there you are. I am the shadow of a cloud. A sudden shower, and then the sun will light the place where I lived. To hell with it. Winner loses. I built the firm that is destroying us. There is nothing to regret. (*Pause.*) Franz, would you like to go for a fast drive? It will toughen you up for war.

FRANZ: Shall we take the Porsche?

FATHER: Certainly. I'll go and bring it from the garage. Wait for me.

FRANZ: Will you give me the signal?

FATHER: The headlights? Yes. (*Pause.*) Leni and Johanna are on the terrace. Say goodbye to them.

FRANZ: I . . . All right. Call them.

FATHER: See you in a moment, my boy. (*He goes out, and he can be heard offstage as he calls*) Johanna! Leni!

(FRANZ *approaches the mantelpiece and looks at his photograph. Suddenly he snatches off the crape and throws it on the floor.*)

LENI (*appearing on the threshold*): What are you doing?

FRANZ (*laughing*): I'm alive, aren't I?

(JOHANNA *enters.* FRANZ *comes downstage.*)

LENI: You're in civilian clothes, lieutenant?

FRANZ: Father is driving me to Hamburg, and I shall take the boat tomorrow. You will never see me again. You have won, Johanna. Werner is free. Free as air. Good luck. (*He is near the table. He places his fore-*

finger on the tape recorder.) I make you a gift of my tape recorder. With my best recording—December seventeenth, fifty-three. I was inspired. You will listen to it later—someday when you want to know the case for the defense, or when you merely want to recall my voice. Do you accept it?

JOHANNA: I accept.

FRANZ. Goodbye.

JOHANNA: Goodbye.

FRANZ: Goodbye, Leni. (*He caresses her hair in the same way as the* FATHER *did.*) Your hair is soft.

LENI: Which car are you taking?

FRANZ: Yours.

LENI: Which road are you taking?

FRANZ: The Elbe Embankment.

(*Two car lights shine outside, lighting up the room through the French windows.*)

LENI: I see. Father is signaling you. Goodbye.

(FRANZ *goes out. There is the sound of a car engine, which grows louder, then fades away. The headlights sweep the French windows as the car goes past.*)

LENI: What time is it?

JOHANNA (*who is nearer the clock*): Six thirty-two.

LENI: At six thirty-nine my Porsche will be in the water. Goodbye!

JOHANNA (*taken aback*): Why?

LENI: Because the Teufelsbrücke is seven minutes from here.

JOHANNA: They are going to . . .

LENI: Yes.

JOHANNA (*hard and tense*): You have killed him!

LENI (*just as hard*): And you? (*Pause.*) What does it matter? He didn't want to live.

JOHANNA (*still in control of herself, but on the verge of breaking down*): Seven minutes.

LENI (*going up to the clock*): Six now. No, five and a half.

JOHANNA: Can't we do anything?

LENI (*still hard*): Bring them back? Try. (*Pause.*) What are you going to do now?

JOHANNA (*trying to control herself*): Werner will decide that. And you?

LENI (*pointing to* FRANZ's *room*): Someone must occupy that room. It shall be me. I won't see you any more, Johanna. (*Pause.*) Be good enough to tell Hilda to knock on that door tomorrow morning I shall give her my orders. (*Pause.*) Still two minutes. (*Pause.*) I did not hate you. (*She walks over to the tape recorder.*) The case for the defense. (*She opens the tape recorder.*)

JOHANNA: I don't want to . . .

LENI: Seven minues! Don't bother!—They're dead.

(*She presses the button of the tape recorder immediately after her last words.* FRANZ's *voice is heard almost at once.* LENI *crosses the room while* FRANZ *is speaking. She climbs the stairs and enters the room.*)

VOICE OF FRANZ (*from the tape recorder*): Centuries of the future, here is my century, solitary and deformed—the accused. My client is tearing himself open with his own hands. What you take for white lymph is blood. There are no red corpuscles, for the accused is dying of hunger. But I will tell you the secret of these multiple incisions. The century might have been a good one had not man been watched from time immemorial by the cruel enemy who had sworn to destroy him, that hairless, evil, flesh-eating beast—man himself. One and one make one—there's our mystery. The beast was hiding, and suddenly we surprised his look deep in the eyes of our neighbors. So we struck. Legitimate self-defense. I surprised the beast. I struck. A man fell, and in his dying eyes I saw the beast still living—myself. One and one make one—what a misunderstanding! Where does it come from, this rancid, dead taste in my mouth? From man? From the beast? From myself? It is the taste of the century. Happy centuries, you who do not know our hatreds, how could you understand the atrocious power of our fatal loves? Love. Hatred. One and one. . . . Acquit us! My client was the first to know shame. He knows he is naked. Beautiful children, you who are born of us, our pain has brought you forth. This century is a woman in labor. Will you condemn your mother? Eh? Answer! (*Pause.*) The thirtieth century no longer replies. Perhaps there will be no more centuries after ours. Perhaps a bomb will blow out all the lights. Everything will be dead—eyes, judges, time. Night. Oh, tribunal of the night—you who were, who will be, and who are—I have been! I have been! I, Franz von Gerlach, here in this room, have taken the century upon my shoulders and have said: "I will answer for it. This day and forever." What do you say?

(LENI *has entered* FRANZ'S *room.* WERNER *appears at the door of the house.* JOHANNA *sees him and goes toward him. Their faces are expressionless. They go out without speaking. From* FRANZ'S *words:* "Eh? Answer!" *the stage is empty.*)

CURTAIN